SEE HER

SMILE

How You Can Make Her Happy
More Often

Adam Khan

Publisher: Free Woman Press
Printed in the United States

ISBN-13: 978-1623815028
ISBN-10: 1623815029

If you ever have any questions or comments about anything in this book, or anything at all, I encourage you to contact me at adamlikhan@mail.com.

Dedication

Men the world over who care about the woman they love, who try to make her happy and have the terrible feeling they are continually failing, without knowing what they're doing wrong, I salute your noble intentions and all the unsung actions you take on love's behalf. This book is dedicated to you. When your good intentions are combined with the know-how within these pages, everyone's dream comes true. Let's make it happen.

Table of Contents

Acknowledgment

The one person who has taught me the most about relationships and how to be happy — and for the most part, taught me against my will — is my wife, Klassy Evans. She is in the 99th percentile of honest people, a fierce warrior for love, a brilliant woman, and the most courageous human being I have ever known. I want to thank her here officially for never giving up on me.

The Juice in Life

You already know about adrenaline and cortisol. Known as "stress hormones," their job is to put your body into high gear, making you ready to fight or flee. But your body also needs downtime. Just as you must both workout *and* rest in order to build muscle, the body needs some way to balance the adrenaline-cortisol fight-or-flight system in order to stay healthy.

And your body has such a system. Oxytocin is a hormone that makes you feel calm, relaxed and affectionate, speeds healing, and promotes bonding, closeness, and trust.

Some side-effects of oxytocin are lower stress, better face-reading, more open communication, feelings of connection, and feeling less isolated. Oxytocin also reduces pain and increases sociability.

Oxytocin makes you feel contented. When your body is saturated with oxytocin, you have a gentle, blissful feeling of completeness. In that moment, you don't need or want anything.

Now all this time you have been relating to the woman you love, she has wanted something from you and sometimes you haven't known or understood what she wanted. But when you understand what oxytocin is and what it does, you'll finally realize how you can make her happy.

She wants *oxytocin*. She may not know the name of it or even know it exists, but that's what she wants. She wants to feel close to you, to bond with you, to connect with you, to know you and she wants you to know her, she wants to trust you, to feel safe and loved.

What she wants from you is *real* — it's a hormone our own bodies produce. It's a state of mind and body produced by oxytocin. And it's good for her and good for *you*. It's good for your health — both of you, but it is also good for you emotionally and psychologically. It makes you both happier.

What she wants is *good*.

Now the bad news: Testosterone *impedes* oxytocin in your body. And estrogen *enhances* oxytocin's effects. Since you have ten to twenty times more testosterone in your body than she does, and she has far more estrogen in her body than you do, she is more tuned into oxytocin. She's far more aware of the value of connecting and bonding and trusting. She understands oxytocin far better than you ever will. But it is in *both* your best interests to have more of it. And you can.

There are things you can *do* that cause your bodies (hers and yours) to release more oxytocin into your blood stream. These things will sound very familiar because they are things she wants you to do. She may hint, she may beg, she may demand, or she may keep it to herself (yet long for it), but she has probably made it clear to you that she wants more of these things.

What she wants is oxytocin. Here are some things you can do that will cause her body to release more of it into her blood stream (and will simultaneously do the same for you):

- Hug her.

- Listen to her talk about whatever she wants to talk about, giving her the gift of your attention and interest.

- Confess to her something that's been on your mind — good or bad.

- Give her a massage.

- Go for an easy walk with her and talk honestly about whatever thoughts and feelings you have.

- Hold her hand.

- Ask her something about her life, or how she feels, or what's on her mind. Try to get to know her better.

- Tell her you love her.

- Show her you love her and care about her. Demonstrate it in some way.

These are a few of the many things you can do that raise the blood levels of oxytocin in both of you.

What do all these things have in common? They are things that make the two of you feel closer to each other.

She wants to feel close to you. She wants *you* to feel close to *her*. And some of the things she does that may have confused you before were only motivated by her desire for that closeness and trust and intimacy, and because she knows better than you what it takes to feel close to someone, you might not have understood what she was doing or why. She naturally knows better than you that the feeling of closeness is valuable and important. Her body is more aware of it and more sensitive to it, and she has been aware of it all her life, so she is far more familiar with it.

In addition to the things on that list, *sex* raises oxytocin levels in the blood. It is also true that rising oxytocin levels makes sex more desirable to her, and more enjoyable. And during a climax, the human body is flooded with oxytocin.

The "buzz" of oxytocin is subtle, but familiar and distinct. You've been under its influence many times, starting with birth. It is the flow of oxytocin from the fetus into the mother's body that starts labor in the first place. In fact, to artificially induce labor, doctors inject Pitocin — a synthetic oxytocin. But even during natural childbirth, both mother and child are filled with an abundant amount of oxytocin, causing them to bond instantly with each other. Oxytocin is the "bonding hormone."

When I was first learning about this stuff, I had an experience that taught me to recognize what oxytocin feels like. Klassy had just given me a long massage and

I was getting into the shower afterwards. I had this wonderful feeling. I was trying to describe it to myself. I felt…

I couldn't put it in words. I just felt so…happy, at peace, content, but something more. What was it?

And finally I found the word: I felt *loved.* That's oxytocin. It's a great feeling.

Joy Nordenstrom, the creator, owner and CEO of JoyofRomance.com, who hosts romantic dinner parties and "coaches clients on how to be more romantic," attended an "oxytocin party," where people took oxytocin lozenges. Nordenstrom filmed the party and walked around interviewing the attendees while they were "high" on oxytocin. We are *not* talking about the addictive drug, OxyContin, by the way. *Oxytocin* is a natural hormone your body releases. OxyContin is something entirely different and unrelated.

It was interesting to hear people trying to describe what oxytocin feels like. One woman said, "It's a hard feeling to describe. Almost like I'm a little drunk, but just in a happy way."

Another woman said, pointing to the man next to her, "We had an argument on Sunday, and it left me pretty upset. By Tuesday when Mark had given me two of them (oxytocin lozenges), it was all gone. And I was just like curled up next to him throughout the rest of the night. Like I couldn't fathom fighting at all."

Nordenstrom took two lozenges herself and after an hour she said, "I feel just an overall feeling of well-being, and like I said — the smile — like perma-grin …It's a good feeling."

If you're interested in watching the video, you can see it here:

http://blip.tv/intelligent-love-411-for-men-/oxytocin-party-1632965

Joy Nordenstrom wrote, "Literally translated in Greek to 'quick birth,' the neurotransmitter oxytocin (ox-ee-TOE-sin) is naturally released in women's bodies during childbirth, breastfeeding, nipple stimulation and orgasm. It is found in equal amounts in both men and women but its affects are felt more by women because of their levels of estrogen and prolactin, which increase the effects. Testosterone in men has the opposite effect…Its presence in the body is associated with an increase in recognizing facial cues, bonding, the reduction of anxiety and an overall increase in levels of trust. As part of its anti-anxiety effects, it also helps relax and reduce blood pressure and cortisol levels. In men, oxytocin may facilitate healthy erections and sperm ejaculation."

Studies also show that oxytocin improves your ability to read faces. In one experiment, Siri Leknes at the University of Oslo gave students a nasal spray that contained either oxytocin or salt water and then they were shown photos of people with happy, angry or neutral expressions on their faces. But some of the facial expressions in these photos were subtle and not easily recognized by most people. Those who had received the oxytocin were better able to read the more subtle expressions than those who received salt water. This is only one of many experiments showing that oxytocin improves the ability to recognize emotions in others.

Oxytocin increases your empathy for others. This improves your ability to connect with people. It increases your feeling of closeness with your woman, and that's what she wants — a feeling of closeness.

One of the things that most easily and directly creates an oxytocin release is *touch*.

Physical Touch

In the 1960's, Sydney Jourard did an experiment to find out how often people touched each other in different countries. His study consisted of going to cities around the world and simply counting how many times people touched each other while sitting together in a cafe.

In Paris, the average was 110 times an hour. In San Juan (a city in Puerto Rico) — the highest average of any city — people touched each other 180 times per hour! In Florida, it was twice per hour, which wasn't quite as bad as London, where they didn't touch at all.

Have we improved how much we touch each other since then? I don't know. But regardless of what the *average* is, you personally can do more touching.

Being touched raises your woman's oxytocin level, and it will raise your own at the same time. Studies show *getting* a massage raises your oxytocin level considerably, but so does *giving* a massage.

Even being *in the same room* with someone who has an elevated oxytocin level will elevate your own. Researchers aren't sure yet how this happens, but they have discovered *that* it happens. It might be something released in the air when oxytocin levels rise.

Another interesting feature of oxytocin is that it can create a positive or negative self-enhancing cycle. When you don't get touched much, your oxytocin level is low, and when it's low, you *don't want* to be touched.

Think about the consequences here. The more your woman's oxytocin level goes up, the more she likes being touched and wants to be touched. Touching then raises her oxytocin even more. It's a positive, upward cycle.

Start today adding more touch into your daily life. Give her massages. A good way to learn how to give a massage is to get a DVD showing you how to do it. There are some good instructional videos on YouTube too.

The physical effects of massage (such as relaxing muscles and moving lymph fluid) are good for your health, but the rise in your oxytocin level may be even better for your health — recent research has shown a rise in oxytocin not only lowers stress, it improves *immune* function, and speeds up the repair of physical injuries. Wounds heal faster, and oxytocin reduces inflammation.

Massage is a powerful oxytocin-raiser. But even on a smaller and more casual scale, you can touch more and it will make a difference. Any touch that feels good raises oxytocin. Hold hands. Put your arm around her. Hug. When you sit and talk, be in physical contact.

Seeking to Accomplish

Because you're male, you are more tuned to action and getting things done than you are to feeling close to her. So sometimes her desire to be close to you might annoy you. She wants long, rambling conversations about what seems like nothing in particular (or just "complaints") and you just want it to be over as soon as possible so you can do something more important or more fun. Up until now you didn't understand what she was trying to do with those conversations.

It's not your fault. You are under the influence of testosterone, a wonderful hormone with lots of great effects. It builds muscle, reduces fat, makes you feel confident and energetic, creates your sex drive, etc.

Testosterone makes you feel good. But it has its downsides too. And one of them is that it impedes oxytocin in your body. This must have been helpful for survival a hundred thousand years ago, so that's the way our bodies evolved. But if you want to be happy, if you want *her* to be happy, you need to recognize that you have a deficiency, and let her guide you. It's good for both of you.

If you have ever had a good hunting dog, you know dogs have much better noses than people do. A bloodhound can detect and distinguish smells at least a *thousand times* better than humans.

So if you're hunting with your dog, *you let the dog guide you.* The bitch can detect things you can't detect. If you let the dog lead, you will both be happy. If *you* insist on leading, you'll *both* end up not getting what you want.

Something similar is true with your woman. She can detect things you *can't* detect, or things you can only detect poorly. She detects these things strongly and *with certainty*. And because she has been under the influence of *estrogen* all her life, which enhances oxytocin's effects, she has gotten very good at tuning into the feeling of oxytocin, very good at noticing its effects, noticing what causes it to rise and fall, and very good at getting close to people.

She's in another league. The distance between her sensitivity and yours may very well be as great as the difference between the nose of a bloodhound and a the nose of a human.

So pay attention to what she's saying, even if you want to automatically discount what she's saying as not important. Connection *is* important. Love *is* important. Even to you.

Remember it with this phrase: *Respect the bitch.* It will help you remember the analogy with the dog. And if that word ever occurs to you (as in, "she's being a bitch") you will have a different meaning — she's being a bitch, so she is perceiving something important that you are oblivious to. But also, it means "respect the specific complaint." Respect the bitch.

Two researchers, in a report in Harvard Business Review, discovered something you should remember. The researchers, in the course of their 30 years of research, had already identified 16 of the most important competencies a leader should have, such as practicing self-development, driving for results, and innovation. But their latest study compared men and women leaders and found that women were rated higher by their peers and bosses on 15 of the 16 competencies. That means that women are better leaders. This seems so completely counterintuitive to a man, it would be easy to dismiss. Of course, we can't conclude from this that all women are better leaders than all men, because all the people in the survey were organizational leaders already. But it does say that when they are leaders, they are exceptionally good at those characteristics that make a good leader.

Another unrelated study by the research firm Catalyst found that organizations with three or more women sitting on their board of directors donated — are you ready for this? — *28 times* more money to charity than corporations with no women board members!

Yet another study found that corporations with women on their boards were more successful when challenged by difficult economic conditions than corporations with men-only boards.

But you are in a relationship, not an organization. And neither of you are the "leader." You're in a partership, which is a different thing altogether. However, some of the same characteristics that would make a good partner would also make a good leader. So all I'm saying here is to listen to her. Give her the respect she deserves. Try, as much as your male brain can do it, to embrace her as a partner, with neither of you being "the leader" and neither being the follower. This isn't going to be easy for you. You have a male mind. It naturally thinks in hierarchies. One must be over the other. "Either you be the boss, or *I* will." That's the way your mind thinks — partnership is more challenging for a man.

Love is at *least* as important as accomplishment and making a difference in the world. There have been times in your life when you understood this great truth. But the rest of the time, your testosterone keeps you focused on other things. Testosterone allows you to set love and connection aside "for now" so you can focus on what you're doing. Testosterone tends to push you out of balance if you aren't consciously preventing it.

She does not have this advantage (or problem, depending on circumstances). She is speaking from a body acutely sensitized to what is truly important in life far more often than you are.

So listen to her. Try to connect with her. Try to give her what she wants (closeness). You will both live a life you are more satisfied with.

Fill the Love Tank

In Gary Chapman's book, *The Five Love Languages*, he says when you can speak your woman's love language, you fill her "love tank." (You'll learn more about love languages in the next chapter.)

When your woman feels loved, it puts her in a great mood. And when her love tank is full, she wants to fill *your* tank.

But when her tank is empty, when she doesn't *feel* loved, she doesn't want to do much for you. People are giving when they feel loved. And much less so when they don't.

This "love tank" analogy is a fairly accurate description of the effect of oxytocin. When her oxytocin level is high, she feels loving. She wants to touch and be touched. When it's low, she doesn't feel loving, and she doesn't want to touch or be touched.

You fill her tank by raising her oxytocin. Speaking your woman's love language can really help. What you put out in this way will come back to you in kind. Speaking your spouse's love language is a gift. Give in this way, and you will receive in abundance.

Why the Emphasis on Being Responsible?

You may have noticed your woman gets particularly stressed by anything you do that seems irresponsible. This is also motivated by her desire for oxytocin. Feeling close is comforting and soothing. It's a feeling of trust and safety. When you act irresponsibly, it makes her feel she can't trust you, and if she can't trust you, it makes her less willing to feel close to you. It prevents her oxytocin response from working.

A man's natural response to his woman bitching about responsibility is "chill out, relax, and quit being so high strung." But that is only because he doesn't understand the purpose of trust in her way of thinking. She wants to feel close to you, and that is not something to dismiss casually. Testosterone makes you so naturally alienated from the whole connection process, you don't even know why she seems so fixated on your responsibility. But maybe now you will understand it differently.

I keep saying bad things about testosterone, but you should know, I love testosterone. It just interferes with connection. In many other ways, however, it is a great hormone. First of all, it makes us feel good. People who take artificial testosterone injections report that it makes them more energetic, more confident, and boosts their mood. It reduces fat and increases muscle. It increases the sex drive. It makes you feel more motivated. There are lots of good things about it, but it also has its downside, which you can compensate for if you know about it and know what to do.

The Opposite of Stress

Feeling alone can be stressful. Isolation is stressful. But feeling connected is soothing and comforting. Part of the reason is the effect of oxytocin. It counterbalances the effects of the stress hormones, adrenaline and cortisol.

In ancient times, humans got plenty of connection. Our ancestors' lives were *filled* with connection. But now the modern world works against it, constantly isolating us from each other. That causes more stress than necessary.

Because you live in a Western society in the 21st century, you have a problem. If you were born 100 years ago or 2000 or 50,000 years ago, you would probably be a member of a small, tight-knit group of people you had known all your life. Almost nobody would ever move away, and you would probably have lived in the same place with the same group of people your entire life. Everybody you knew as a child would still be around and you would see them every day.

There would be, of course, no computers, no televisions — in fact, you would have very few forms of entertainment other than interacting with people you knew well.

You would have moved to a natural rhythm. No alarm clocks or time pressures or calendars. No schedule books.

Times have changed, haven't they? Many of the changes have created more stress and loneliness and feelings of isolation than could ever have been possible in the past.

Most of us don't even know the names of our next door neighbors. You go off to work, away from your family, away from your neighborhood. You live a separate life, even from the people you live with. Almost all of us are in the same situation. Our families have moved all over the country. We don't even know where most of our old school chums are now. And we have more forms of entertainment than we know what to do with, and they aggressively compete for our attention. According to surveys and census reports, 14 to 15 percent of Americans move to another *community* in any given year. According to the Census Bureau, about 7½ percent of us move to another *address* every year. Only one fourth of U.S. teens expect to live in their hometowns when they grow up.

Even during the little time we actually spend with people we love, we are usually doing things like watching television and movies — we're together, but we're not getting any closer to each other.

Being close to people used to be natural and inevitable. You almost couldn't avoid having strong, close ties with many people. Times have changed. If you are going to have close relationships with people, you will have to do it deliberately. The circumstances no longer make it inevitable.

What do you think happens when you isolate an extremely social animal like a human being? You get depression, anxiety, stress, alienation, loneliness, alcoholism, etc., without ever recognizing that the source of these troubles is a lack of connection. The depressed or anxious thoughts a person has may be about work or self-esteem or about anything really, and no doubt people have been having thoughts like that throughout the ages. But what we no longer have is a tight-knit community of people we can talk openly to, or just comfortably be with. We don't have that buffering effect any more.

Feeling isolated, all by itself, causes negative feelings, which can cause you to obsess about what might be bothering you. But you may not correctly identify isolation as the cause. You might think of many other things to be upset about. But trying to fix those problems won't cure your negative feelings. What will make you feel better is feeling connected with others.

You *can* get closer to people, even in this society, and it can have an enormous impact on your health and on your general feeling of well-being and happiness.

The circumstances are stressing us out, but the balancing part, the soothing, calming part is not as easily available as it used to be.

But you can make it available to you and your woman. You can work around the barriers modernity puts up between us. And if you do, you'll feel calmer and happier, and you'll be healthier.

Dean Ornish found that one of the most effective treatments he provides (in his program that actually reverses the heart disease of his patients — not just slowing it or stopping it, but *reversing* it) is teaching his patients to connect better with their spouse and kids. You can (and should) read more about this in Ornish's book, *Love and Survival.*

Studies have been coming down the pike in huge abundance for many years that one of the most important causes of happiness is good relationships. Closeness. Happy people are close to others. The more isolated or alienated a person is — no matter how wealthy he is or how much exercise he gets or how great his diet is — the more likely he is to be miserable and unhealthy. Happiness and closeness go together. Unhappiness and isolation go together.

Activating the oxytocin system has some practical consequences. It doesn't just feel good; it doesn't just improve your mood. Connecting causes important physical changes in your body.

Look at it this way: A powerful drug that raises your mood has been discovered, and it's available without a prescription. The drug makes people feel calm and relaxed, trusting, generous, and affectionate. It makes people feel unstressed.

This drug has some odd side-effects, however: It sometimes causes a marked improvement in face-reading, a dramatic opening of communication and feelings of connection, and it makes you feel less isolated. All these results add up to one of the best moods you have ever experienced.

It also reduces pain and improves sociability. It boosts the immune system and speeds healing.

But you don't take the wonder-drug in pill form. It has to be rubbed into your skin. And in fact, the drug is produced by your own body in response to the rubbing. The "drug" is oxytocin.

Good For Your Heart

Cardiovascular specialists can look at several things to figure out a man's chances of having angina (chest pain, usually caused by heart disease). Does he smoke? That will increase his chances. Does he exercise? That will lower his chances. Does he have high cholesterol? And so on.

But a study at Case Western Reserve University showed that one question is a better predictor of angina than any question they've been able to come up with: Does your wife show you her love? The study was done on ten thousand men who did not have any chest pain at the start of the study. The researchers found that even if a man had several risk factors (like high blood pressure and a sedentary lifestyle), if he felt his wife showed him her love, it was protective. He was less likely to have angina.

Men who had the same risk factors but answered "no" had almost twice as much chest pain.

Dean Ornish says researchers approach this question in many different ways, but they all find the same thing. He describes study after study showing the powerful effects of connection on peoples' health, and he summarized it all with this:

> In other words, do you have anyone who really cares for you? Who feels close to you? Who loves you? Who wants to help you? In whom you can confide?
>
> If the answers are no, you may have three to five times higher risk of premature death and disease from all causes — or even higher, according to some studies. These include increased risk of heart attack, stroke, infectious diseases, many types of cancer, allergies, arthritis, tuberculosis, autoimmune diseases, low birth weight and low Apgar scores, alcoholism, drug abuse, suicide, and so on.

The connections you have make a *big* difference. When you feel loved by your woman and when you contribute to and love her, it significantly improves how happy you feel — which you probably know already — but it *also* improves how physically healthy you are.

The Dog Connection

An eleven year-old boy in Canada was gathering fire-wood to bring into the house, just like every other day, when his golden retriever, Angel, began walking next to the boy rather than running around the yard as she usually did.

Suddenly a cougar leapt at the boy from about ten feet away. But the cougar was intercepted mid-charge by Angel as she jumped over a lawn mower to inter-vene. "I was just lucky my dog was there, because it happened so fast I wouldn't have known what hit me," said the boy in an interview afterwards.

The cougar seized Angel's head in its jaws and the boy ran to tell his mother, who called the Mounties, who then saved Angel from the death grip of the cougar. Angel survived.

Stories like this show us the survival value of owning a dog, but there is a much more common effect dogs have: Their presence tends to improve your mood. If you've been on the fence about getting a dog, you should consider this important fact: Having a dog lowers stress and improves your health.

In a press release by International Association of Human-Animal Interaction Organizations, they wrote "The organizers of the 12th International Conference of Human-Animal Interactions have announced that at their meeting this July, scientists will be presenting their latest findings confirming that friendly human-dog interaction releases oxytocin in both human and dog.

"The experiment found that women and their dogs experienced similar increases in oxytocin levels after ten minutes of friendly contact. Also the women's oxytocin response was significantly correlated to the quality of the bond they reported in a survey taken prior to the interacting with their pets."

This is true for men too. When you pet your dog, oxytocin levels rise in both you and your dog. When a human pets someone else's dog, oxytocin rises, but not nearly as much. It is the *love* between the two that causes the big rise.

Since a higher level of oxytocin leads to a desire to touch and be touched, the presence of a dog in your home can keep everyone's oxytocin level raised, and that can have positive long-term consequences on your relationship.

If you'd like to learn more about oxytocin, two books I recommend are *The Oxytocin Factor* by the researcher, Kerstin Uvnas Moberg, and *The Chemistry of Connection* by Susan Kuchinskas.

You've learned what your woman really wants (oxytocin) and you've learned what produces feelings of love and connection for women in general. But now let's explore what is most important to *your* woman in particular. That's the subject of the next chapter.

The Five Love Languages

This idea has really helped me, as simple as it is. I first read about the idea in a book on NLP (a branch of psychology) that said people have three primary "representational systems:" auditory, visual, and kinesthetic. That is, we rely on one sensory mode more than the others, in the same way that we rely on one hand more than the other (being right handed or left handed). For accessing memory, for the way we communicate, for what matters most to us, for what we notice first, for what we feel is most important, we tend to favor one sense over the others.

In other words, someone can be a "visual" person. They rely most on their visual sense. They are tuned into visual information. They store their memories and access these memories easiest *visually*. And when they speak, the words they use are visual — "the way I see it, it has become clear to me, you've got to see the big picture."

If someone is an *auditory* person, they tend to rely on sounds and words for memories and information storage and access. And the words they tend to use are auditory — "that doesn't sound right to me, we just don't click, I really resonate with what you're saying."

And the same goes for a kinesthetic person. They are focused on feelings and physical sensations — "I'm not comfortable with this, it feels dangerous, I have a strong gut reaction."

In the NLP literature, this idea of people favoring one sensory mode over others is primarily used to help therapists talk to their clients in a way that gains and maintains rapport.

So if a therapist was talking to a *visual* client, but the therapist herself was an *auditory* person, they would be speaking different languages, so to speak, and the therapist would have a more difficult time getting rapport with the client. So it was suggested that the therapist favor the *client's* sensory system rather than her own. She should use visual language in her speech, rather than the auditory terms that come naturally to her, in this example. Improving trust and rapport would help the client make changes. Rapport helps the therapist influence the client.

Of course, the same goes for you in your relationship with your woman. It matters what sensory mode your woman favors. You should find out what it is.

And it matters what *you* favor. Often they are not the same. If you favor auditory, you will tend to express your love with words and sounds, and when she *tells* you she loves you or compliments you with words, this will matter more to you and you will remember it better than if she hugs you or holds your hand.

And the same is true the other way. If the sensory mode she favors is visual, then what you *do* for her will matter more to her than what you *say*. You could tell her all the time you love her, you could compliment her until you are blue in the face, and it is perfectly possible for her to not feel loved by you. You're not speaking her "love language."

Gary Chapman took this idea a few steps further.

In his book, *The Five Love Languages*, Chapman says what makes one spouse feel loved might not be what makes the *other* spouse feel loved. And he calls these different ways to feel loved "love languages." According to Chapman, the five love languages are:

> acts of service
> physical touch
> words of affirmation
> quality time
> receiving gifts

In the beginning of every relationship, most of us stop thinking about anything except our new sweetheart. We communicate our affection with *all five* love languages. With such a shotgun approach, we're sure to make each other feel loved.

But as time goes on, your expressions of love tend to streamline, and you eventually drop out every expression of love that isn't valuable to *you*. What you'll have left is the one love language that means the most to you: Your own. If you two just happen to have the same love language, it isn't a problem. But usually that isn't the case.

For example, Dan's love language is words of affirmation. His wife Judy's love language is acts of service.

It has probably never occurred to Dan that people wouldn't appreciate words of affirmation, so his expression has streamlined to mostly *words* — heartfelt words of love and appreciation. When he really wants Judy to know how much he loves her, he *tells* her. Judy likes hearing it, but words alone don't really make her feel loved. The words are nice, but that's all they are to her: nice. They are "just words."

Meanwhile Judy has streamlined *her* expression of love to the one that really counts as far as *she* is concerned: Acts of service. She goes out of her way to take care of Dan. She makes sure the house is always clean, his clothes are always washed and folded with care, etc. She tries to help him out whenever she can. But Dan hardly even notices. What he *does* notice is that Judy almost never *tells* him she loves him anymore. She hardly ever tells him she *believes* in him. She hardly ever whispers in his ear.

Judy's acts of service "fall on deaf ears." He cares very little about how clean the kitchen is. He's not visually tuned in. He rarely even notices (much less appreciates) her many sacrifices and hard work.

It's a tragic irony. Judy is *going way out of her way* to make Dan feel loved, and he goes around resentful that she never tells him she loves him.

Meanwhile, he tries to express himself verbally to let her know how much she means to him, and all she does is complain about how he never helps with the housework and never does the things she asks him to do (she is requesting *acts of service*, and if he did them, she would feel loved). And because Dan favors auditory input, these complaints fall like daggers into his heart, with more pain than similar words would hurt Judy.

Which One is Her Love Language?

Many of us are in a similar situation to Dan and Judy. If this seems all too familiar, the thing to do is to find out what your spouse's love language is, and then learn to express your affection in *that* way instead of in the way *you* value most. It may feel a little awkward at first, as it would to learn a second language of any kind, but use it enough, and it will start to feel more comfortable.

So how do you find out what your woman's love language is?

First, look at how she normally expresses her love for *you*. Although it may not be *your* love language, it's probably hers, since we usually express our love most often in the way we think is most meaningful.

You can also notice what she most often asks for. For example, if she's always suggesting you go for a trip together, or go for a walk, or turn off the television and talk, her love language is probably quality time.

If she's always wanting to hold your hand or complains that you don't touch her enough, and she is always offering to give *you* a massage, her love language is probably physical touch.

Find out what makes her feel loved, and learn to communicate your affection using that love language. And help your mate learn *your* language. After that, you know what to do: Live happily ever after.

There are undoubtedly things about your woman that make you feel overcome with affection for her. Memories of moments you had together, memories of things she has done for you, moments when she stood by you when everyone else didn't, or characteristics about her that you find so endearing that you well up at the thought of them.

Think of one of these — a characteristic of hers or a memory of something that makes you feel a strong feeling of affection and love for her. Now communicate that feeling to her using *her* love language.

What Doesn't Come Naturally

Sometimes when I read something good, I copy the quote or paragraph or page from a book and post it. I have a bulletin board for just that purpose, and I always have something new on the board to re-read (and hopefully sink in). I keep these "postables" in a file and rotate them. One such nugget I've had around a long time is a page from Chapman's book.

On the page is a conversation Chapman had with one of his clients. The client basically said, "Yes, I understand that my spouse's love language is physical touch, but I was never hugged as a child and it's not my language. I'm not a toucher."

I love Chapman's response: "Do you have two hands?" He instructs the client to put his hands together and then imagine his spouse in between. "I'll bet if you hug your spouse three thousand times," he says, "it will begin to feel more comfortable."

Comfort isn't the point, anyway. Love is a *verb*. It's something you *do*. Specifically, acts of love are what you do *for someone else*. We do things all day long that do not come "naturally." And we do them because we want the result. We do them because they're worthwhile. Speaking your woman's love language should be one of them.

This love language idea is very powerful. You can do something *today* that brings her closer to you. You can *do* something that makes you feel more affection for each other. You can do something for her — something she will really appreciate, something that will make her feel loved.

What she will appreciate may not be what comes naturally for you. It doesn't matter. Do you love her? Do you want her to *know* and *feel* your love? Then you should think in terms of what *she* will appreciate rather than what *you* would appreciate if she did it for you, or what "feels most natural" to you.

After awhile, expressing her love language will come more naturally for you, and you may eventually even like it. But that's not as important as it seems.

Think of your woman. Has she ever requested something that you have ignored? Has she ever hinted at something she would like, but since you weren't interested or didn't consider it valuable, you've shined it on? You could make a huge difference in your relationship to reconsider.

Try doing even a little of what doesn't come naturally and notice what happens. It will make both of you happier.

Testosterone: The Good, the Bad and the Ugly

Testosterone is a hormone, and it is having many effects on your body and brain right now. And while you were in utero, it made permanent changes to your brain and body. Some of its effects in utero changed the structure of your brain and altered the way it functions. Some of those changes make it more difficult for you to have a good relationship with your woman. More difficult, but not impossible.

For example, your brain became more compartmentalized during your gestation in the womb. That is, specific parts of your brain do specific things, and other parts do not share that job.

A woman's brain is less compartmentalized. So the effect of a stroke in a particular part of the brain may completely eliminate an ability in a man, but will *not* eliminate it in a woman. If a stroke knocked out the entire left hemisphere of his brain, for example, he would no longer be able to speak. If it did the same to her, she would still be able to speak, but just not as well as she could before.

Another important change made in the womb is in the corpus callosum, the bundle of nerves that connect the left and right hemispheres of the brain, allowing them to communicate. The corpus callosum is smaller in men than in women (even though men's brains are larger than women's). The communication between the two hemispheres of your brain is more restricted because of this.

These physical differences in brain structure help explain why you have a more difficult time putting your feelings into words than she does. Your brain is more compartmentalized, so *only* your left hemisphere can put your feelings into words. And your emotions are processed in your right hemisphere. And the communication between hemispheres is less robust.

Why Such Differences Exist

Nature has done a remarkable thing, and it started a long way back on the evolutionary tree. Evolution found a way to separate the sexes with hormones. This allows the development of two radically different kinds of animals *within the same species*. Any trait that might help the species survive could be developed in one sex but not the other.

Originally, this hormonal separation simply produced the different reproductive organs, but over time, more and more changes have been added, so that now a male deer (buck) has antlers and a female deer does not (for most species of deer), a male peacock has a huge and colorful tail, but the female doesn't, male birds sing, but the females do not.

All these masculine traits are produced by a testosterone-like molecule. Nature found a way to make the male and female versions of the same species have different traits and behavior by making sure masculine traits and behaviors are triggered only by male hormones.

Your body and brain function differently than your woman's body and brain. Some of your masculine traits were built physically in the womb, and some are activated by testosterone in the present — for example, testosterone produces the human sex drive in both men and women, and as it fluctuates, so does your desire for sex.

Most people don't have an appreciation for how many different changes testosterone causes. Let's list a few to give you an idea of how pervasive and fundamental these changes are: Men have thicker skin (not metaphorically, but actually), a thicker skull, a more slanted forehead and heavier brow ridges (to support larger jaw muscles). Men have fewer nerve endings on the surface of our skin, tighter joints, better daytime vision, and better depth perception. And, of course, more muscle.

Our blood coagulates faster than women's. And here's an astonishing difference: In every drop of blood, you have about a *million* more red blood cells than she does!

You can see that most of these differences would give an advantage in a physical combat and in the often dangerous and strenuous pursuit of hunting.

Some researchers thought this was very interesting, and it seemed self-explanatory that these gender differences would come about because of the usual division of labor in hunter-gatherers. In almost every hunter-gatherer society studied, men did almost all the hunting and women did most of the gathering, and there is good evidence to support the idea that it has always been that way with humans and pre-humans.

But sometimes what seems "obvious" is wrong, so these researchers wanted to test the theory. They thought along these lines: "Okay, so men have better depth perception and hit a target with a projectile better than women (which is true). That makes sense for a hunter. What skills or abilities might *gatherers* have evolved?"

They thought, "How about remembering the locations of things?" Wouldn't that be a great skill for a gatherer? To remember where that berry patch was that had so many berries last season? Or where that walnut tree is?

So they tried to find out if women were superior in this skill. In one of their experiments, they piled a bunch of random objects on a large table — a tennis racket, a comb, a book, a hammer, etc. One large pile of random things.

Then they brought people into the room one at a time and had them look at this pile for a specified length of time. Then the person was escorted out of the room. One of the objects was then moved to a different place in the pile, or removed from the room altogether.

The person was brought back in and asked if the pile looked any different. Sure enough, women consistently did significantly better than men. Women are better at remembering the location of things.

I watched another experiment (it was filmed) that showed this difference dramatically. Subjects showed up for an experiment they volunteered for, and the researcher said, "We're not quite ready. Would you please wait in this room while we finish preparing to do the experiment?"

The subject went into a small, cluttered room with nothing in it but a chair and a shelf strewn with things.

After a specified length of time, the subject was brought out and asked, "What was in that room?" That was the whole experiment. What would people notice and remember from being in that room without being asked ahead of time to notice or remember anything?

The differences between the sexes were extreme. Women remembered lots of detail. They named almost everything in the room. And while they were describing it, they were actually demonstrating with their hands that they remembered not just *what* was in there, but the *location* of each item in the room. They would usually start at one end of the shelf and just describe everything: "There was a pack of Wrigley's Spearmint gum with two pieces missing. Next to that was a blue backpack with a book sticking out of it; a book on traveling in the Sierra Mountains. Sticking out from underneath the backpack was a black comb about six inches long with one of its teeth missing," etc.

The men said things like, "There was a bunch of stuff in there, I don't know. A backpack and some other things."

Women are universally more observant, except for things that a man, in his more focused and compartmentalized world, has deemed important.

In fact, women are better at almost all forms of perception. They can distinguish smaller differences in color shades, hear smaller changes in tone of voice and volume, they have better perception of high frequencies, a better ability to distinguish different tastes, more nerve endings in their skin (so they have greater sensitivity to touch), they're better at seeing in the dark, and have superior peripheral vision.

Estrogen activates olfactory receptors, and since women have far more estrogen than men, women have a better sense of smell than men.

Some of these differences probably evolved to make women better *gatherers*, but some of them make women better *mothers*. Hearing a small change in the tone of a baby's cry, seeing a small change in the color of a baby, feeling a small change in the movement or temperature of a baby — all of these probably helped their babies to survive in more primitive times. And probably still help today.

All these superiorities in perception, along with her brain's different structure, give her a significant edge in her ability to connect with others. She is far better at communicating and connecting than you are.

She not only has these physical, perceptual superiorities, but she has estrogen and oxytocin working on her, orienting her interests and attention, focusing her attention on relationships, and that influence has been there her whole life, helping to build and refine her connection skills. To say she is better at connecting than you is to greatly understate the difference. When it comes to relating, the differences between you are immense and extensive.

Of course, all the specific perceptual differences, and all the differences between the sexes I'm listing here are *generalizations*, so in any particular trait and for any particular person, the generalization may not apply. Some men undoubtedly hear higher frequencies than some women, just as some women are taller than some men. But in general, most of these differences will apply to you and your woman.

Your Active Brain

One of the differences between you has a significant effect on your relationship and your ability to deal with conflict: When men are upset, the part of our brains that becomes most active — the part that gets flooded with blood — is the part responsible for moving muscles and coordinating physical action. When you are upset, your system is gearing you up for *doing something.*

When she is upset, the parts of her brain that get the most blood flow are responsible for communicating.

So when the two of you get upset, she is geared up to *talk*; you are geared up to *do* something.

During an argument between a husband and wife, her blood pressure rises, on average, six percent. His rises more than twice as much — on average, fourteen percent.

Your body floods itself with adrenaline and cortisol, the fight or flight hormones. Her body floods itself with less of those, plus her body secretes the counter-hormone, oxytocin — the connecting, calming hormone, the "tend and befriend" hormone.

When something is upsetting, she is *much* better equipped to deal with non-violent, interpersonal conflict. You are much better equipped to deal with physical combat, to establish dominance, and to exert yourself physically.

Remember, testosterone *interferes* with oxytocin, impeding its calming, connecting effects. Estrogen, on the other hand, *enhances* the effects of oxytocin.

You could put it this way: Testosterone impedes your ability to cooperate and it enhances your ability to compete.

In an experiment with rats, researchers set up a condition where two rats could either cooperate with each other or not. If they *could* cooperate, they would be rewarded with sugar water.

The researchers tested four kinds of pairs — pairs of females, pairs of males, pairs of castrated males, and pairs of castrated males given testosterone supplements.

The female pairs cooperated with each other and accomplished the task easily. The same was true for the castrated males.

The normal males and the castrates taking testosterone supplements learned more slowly, and some pairs were not able to cooperate at all, even though it would have been in each of their own best interests. They were too busy trying to establish dominance.

Something similar happens to human beings. Testosterone blinds you, in a sense, to what is most important to you — love. Testosterone changes your focus and interests. To some degree, it overrides what you naturally care about— connecting and cooperating with your woman.

Certain kinds of experiences raise your testosterone level: Participating in, or watching violence, for example. Watching football games, boxing or MMA matches will raise your testosterone. Winning at something raises your testosterone level. Fighting does too, of course. And thinking about sex and having sex raise your testosterone level.

Both men and women in positions of power have measurably higher testosterone levels than people in the lower ranks. This is true for monkeys too, and in fact, when researchers give a small, low-ranking monkey a big dose of testosterone every day, he becomes so aggressive, he fights his way to the top of the monkey hierarchy by sheer scrappiness.

Testosterone is an *aggression* hormone. It is good for competing, but not so good for cooperating and connecting. The research makes this very clear.

The higher the testosterone level in a man, the more prone he is to antisocial behavior, fighting, arrests, and divorce. In a study that matched relationship histories with testosterone levels of more than four thousand men, those with higher testosterone levels were less likely to marry and more likely to divorce.

Interruptions

One specific area where your higher level of aggression shows up daily and strains your relationship is your tendency to interrupt when she is speaking. Or when *anyone* is speaking. Men interrupt far more often than women. To whatever degree you can, try to curb this tendency in yourself. You won't be perfect at it. But you don't have to be perfect to make a difference.

In fact, I'll tell you right now, I am not perfect at any of these things I am suggesting in this book. But if you only do these things *more often*, even a *little* more often, you will see her smile more often.

Interrupting is a great example. If you make an effort and merely interrupt her *less* — if you interrupt her today only five times instead of six — it makes a difference. It helps your relationship. Do the best you can and don't beat yourself up if you can't do it perfectly. You will never be perfect at any of this, but that doesn't matter. Every little bit will help.

When you interrupt her when she's speaking, even when you don't mean it, you are giving the impression that what *you* have to say is more important than what *she* has to say. That is the most basic conclusion any bystander could make about it, and the obvious conclusion she will draw from it too. So every time you interrupt her, you invalidate her. You are dominating her. And you are making lies out of your statements that she is important to you.

She has been talking to men her whole life, so she is probably used to it and may not even notice it, but every day over and over, you keep "telling her" that you don't care about what she says.

To curb this tendency will take effort on your part. Your desire to say what you want to say is very strong. But you love her, and you want her to feel heard. You want her to feel valid and equal. You want her to know you care about what she says. One way to do that is to interrupt her less often.

One of the reasons you interrupt her is that you're afraid if you don't interrupt, you'll forget the vitally important point that you really want to say. Can you live with that for her sake? If what you wanted to say was *really* that important, it will probably come to mind again.

And it's also true that *she* has things to say and if you interrupt her, she can forget what she was going to say too.

Sometimes it will be true that what you have to say is more important than what she has to say. But try to keep it to a minimum for the sake of your connection, for the sake of love, and for the sake of fairness.

Not Optional

You want to care about her and make her feel loved. You think that would be nice, don't you? And she deserves it. But that way of thinking is all wrong. She doesn't *deserve* it, she *needs* it.

If you had a dog, would you decide to give the dog food and water because the dog *deserves* it? No, you feed the dog because you are responsible and you care about the dog and the dog *needs* food.

In your categorical brain, this distinction makes a difference. You need to take "providing oxytocin for her" and move it in your mind from the category, "would be nice" to the category, "a necessity." Then you will be thinking correctly. Then you will give those hugs and time to connect the importance they deserve.

People can *die* from a lack of love. In fact, they die all the time from it. People who don't feel loved die earlier from all causes than people who feel loved. It is a *need*, not just something nice. This is something you should take very seriously.

Connecting, listening, touching — these give *life*. They will give her energy and happiness and a life worth living.

And this is definitely one of those things where what you give comes back to you multiplied. When you make her feel loved, she will make *you* feel loved, and that gives *you* energy and life, and is good for your health.

You Care About Love Too

Viktor Frankl wrote about an experience he had one morning when he was in one of Hitler's concentration camps. He was marching through the snow on his way to a site where he would have to work hard all day in the bitter cold, wearing insufficient clothing, severely underfed, constantly and brutally abused, not knowing if or when he would ever see a normal life, feeling about as low and hopeless and depressed as a person can feel — and then he thought of his wife. He didn't even know if she was alive. He saw her in his mind's eye, and she smiled at him. He wrote:

> For the first time in my life I saw the truth as it is set into song by so many poets, proclaimed as the final wisdom by so many thinkers. The truth — that love is the ultimate and the highest goal to which man can aspire...I understood how a man who has nothing left in this world may still know bliss, be it only for a brief moment, in the contemplation of his beloved.

Although testosterone can dampen your interest in connecting and can impede your ability to communicate and cooperate, *you still care* about these things. She is more in tune with the value of connection and her body and brain is more equipped for it and oriented to it. So she pushes for love and connection. But what you need to realize is that although *she* is pushing for it, it won't just make *her* happier. It will make *you* happier too.

In Dean Ornish's book, *Love and Survival*, he writes about what a difference it makes to men when they finally learn to communicate and connect.

Ornish runs a clinic for people who have already had a heart attack and who are committed to trying to postpone the second one.

It has always been considered inevitable that if you have had one heart attack, you *will* have another, and eventually you'll have one that kills you.

Dean Ornish's program was the first to demonstrate that heart disease can be *reversed*. Not just slowed. Reversed. Those plaque-clogged arteries can actually become progressively less clogged over time.

His program involves yoga and a vegetarian diet, but Ornish asserts that one of the most important elements of his program is that he teaches these men (almost all his patients are men) how to connect with their wives, and makes sure they do it. And in the book he presents a compelling collection of studies that support his assertion that getting these men to connect and communicate openly with their loved ones is one of the most effective things they can do to reverse their heart disease.

Ornish points out that many of these men have spent their lives focusing on their career. Remember, testosterone impedes your desire to connect and enhances your desire to win and compete. These love their wives, and most of them have thought of their career success as something they did for their wife and family.

Their wives, all this time, have yearned for greater connection and intimacy with their husbands. But the men were always too busy with their work, too driven.

But then he had a heart attack. And he has received this dire diagnosis: "You have heart disease. If you do nothing differently, you will, in all likelihood, die of a heart attack, and often it comes fairly soon."

This news sometimes radically changes his priorities. He becomes more open to suggestion than perhaps he has ever been in his adult life. He does not want his life to end so soon.

He shows up at Ornish's clinic and Ornish says, "We can help you but you are going to have to do things differently. And part of that will involve going to classes to teach you to communicate and connect better with the people you love."

These guys are desperate. They would do *anything*. They are even willing to set aside their obsession with winning and change the way they communicate.

After they've gone through the clinic, Ornish says they often come back years later and tell him that they are happier than they have ever been in their lives because of their newfound ability to connect with the people they love.

Testosterone may impede our ability to connect, but it doesn't impede love's capacity to make us happy. It doesn't stop us from knowing deep in the heart of us that love is the most important thing in the world.

It is almost a cliché that the last thought of a dying soldier is of his wife. On the battlefield in the Civil War, the Vietnam War, or the war in Afghanistan, the last words a man will utter is, "Tell my wife I love her."

The reason it's a cliché is that it consistently happens when men know they are going to die.

When they're shot on the battlefield and have only minutes to live, when they are given a terminal diagnosis, when they are starving to death or stranded in the desert dying of thirst, this is the last, most important thought men have.

When it comes down to life or death, when nothing else seems to matter, the one thing that survives — even in a man — is a fundamental knowing that love is "the ultimate and the highest goal to which man can aspire."

I just watched a documentary about a devastating tornado that swept through Oklahoma, destroying homes. They were interviewing people immediately after the tornado, sometimes interviewing people who had literally, moments before, crawled out from underneath the rubble that used to be their home. These people had lost their cars, their homes, and almost every possession they had. The most consistent comment they all made was, "It is just stuff. My family is alive, and that's what matters."

Not one person said, "Well, my wife is dead, but at least my house is still standing." Under the more extreme circumstances, it becomes crystal clear what is really more important.

When nothing life-threatening is happening, we have the "luxury" of putting off what is most important in order to fulfill our desire for other things like accumulating "stuff" and accomplishing things. Those things haven't become actually more important to us than love, but we're behaving as if they have, and that's a shame. It's foolish, and we all know it. Let's begin today to stop living a lie. Let's start living our lives consistent with the truth that we know in our hearts.

Yes, accomplishment is wonderful. Yes, winning feels great. Yes, success is important. But you know and I know love is greater than all these.

Testosterone does not destroy our appreciation of love. But it impedes our ability to reach and enjoy the love we could have. And while we may not want to stop testosterone from doing what it does (and short of drugs or surgery couldn't stop it anyway), we can work around it. We can compensate for it. We can do something about it.

And the best thing you can do about it is to begin today turning toward all her bids for connection — the topic of our next chapter.

Turn Toward All Her Bids

This simple rule is going to change your life. If you remember nothing else, remember this one. I'm using the word "bid" here in the sense that the researcher John Gottman, uses it. I will explain what a bid is first, and then I will show you how you can see her smile far more often — and not just smile, but care about you, be devoted to you, and love you with all her heart.

So what is a bid?

A bid is the fundamental element of a relationship.

When two people interact, what is the interaction made of? Strip the conversation of its content, and what are the fundamental elements? What are the building blocks of connection?

John Gottman — one of the most influential researchers who explores what makes marriages succeed or fail — uses what they call "the love lab" for studying couples. The lab is an apartment fixed with two-way mirrors and cameras, where married couples come and spend the weekend while being filmed and observed, and then these films are analyzed carefully. After decades of this kind of painstaking analysis of hundreds of thousands of personal interactions, Gottman discovered an elemental core of connection.

It's something he calls "the bid."

In any interaction, one person "makes a bid for connection." The other person responds to that bid in one of three ways: Turning toward, turning against, or turning away.

These are the fundamental components of connection — between anyone. This is what connection is made of: The bid, and the response to the bid.

This understanding removes the complication and confusion from relationships. Who is talking and what they are talking about can produce an infinite variety of combinations, but underneath it all are these basic components.

People are bidding and responding to bids all the time. But without seeing what's happening, a person's habitual responses to bids (by turning away or turning against them) can discourage further bidding. And the bids people make to others can be made in a way that doesn't encourage *good* responses to the bids — again, sometimes without realizing it.

Fully understanding the concept of "the bid" can greatly improve your capacity to connect with people. So what is a "bid?" It can be anything that invites a response. For example:

"Can you tell me what time it is?"

"Hey, Joe, how's it going?"

"You look great in that color!"

"Are you hungry? Do you want to get a pizza?"

"What are you doing tomorrow?"

"I just saw a great movie called *Date Night*. Have you seen it?"

"I don't feel well."

"I woke up in a great mood this morning."

"Have you got a minute?"

Each of these is a bid for connection. And the other person can respond to the bid by turning away, turning against, or turning toward it. The responses of turning *away* and turning *against* tend to diminish the bidder's desire to keep bidding. For example, you say, "You look great in that color!" She could turn *away* by completely ignoring your statement as if she didn't hear it, or responding with something like, "Do you know what time it is?"

Or she could turn *against* it by saying, "I hate this color," or "What do *you* know about color matching?"

Or, of course, she has the option of turning *toward* your bid by saying, "Thank you!" or "Oh, I'm so glad you said that; I don't usually wear this color but I really liked the dress."

Every interaction you have with your woman is a bid, followed by one of those three kinds of responses. That's all there is. These simple building blocks are the foundation of all relationships.

The secret to better connection with your woman is to turn *toward all* her bids for connection. It also wouldn't hurt to improve your ability to *make* good bids.

What Makes a Good Bid?

The point of all the bidding and responding is to give and receive *emotional* information. This is so important, let me say it another way just to be crystal clear: To connect with your woman, the important thing is to *transmit and receive emotional information*.

So a good bid invites the *other* person to give *you* an emotional disclosure. Volunteering some emotional information *about yourself* is also a good way to bid.

Not all bids or responses might seem to deliver emotional information. If I ask you what time it is and you respond "12:30," it may not seem to convey any *emotional* information. But the *way* I ask and the *way* you respond can, in fact, give us emotional information about each other. I can ask you what time it is in a commanding way, in a friendly way, a depressed way, and many others. You can respond to me in many ways too, while technically giving the same answer.

The important thing is that you begin to see your interactions with your woman as *bids* and *responses to bids*. This will give you a whole new way to understand what's happening and it will make it easier for you to connect with her.

Notice the way you bid, and notice the responses you get, and you will naturally get better at connecting.

Don't focus on what's complicated about it. You are a human being, a social animal, and your brain is exquisitely engineered to learn social information, and it will learn all by itself. All you need to focus on is making good bids, and responding to her bids by turning *toward* them.

You might be wondering how you can turn *toward* a bid if she says something like this: "You are a selfish prick." Can you turn *toward* that? Can you even see that as a bid for connection?

The first step is to see *everything* she says to you as a bid for connection. Assume it is, then *turn toward* it.

You can easily see it that way if you think about it. If she didn't want to connect with you, she wouldn't say anything. If she didn't want to stay connected to you, she wouldn't bother trying to talk about something with you that's bothering her.

But how do you turn *toward* it? Are you sometimes selfish? Probably. Can you see how what you did could at least be *interpreted* as selfish, even if it wasn't? If you can, then you can honestly — and it *has* to be honest — turn *toward* her bid. Here are some possible responses:

1. I would like to become less selfish.

2. I understand why that seems selfish.

3. What did I do that seems selfish?

4. You're right about that, at least sometimes.

5. With your help, maybe I could become less so.

6. Tell me more.

7. How does that make you feel?

8. Thank you for telling me how you feel.

9. I appreciate your honesty.

You could think of many more possible responses. The point is that *whatever* she says, take it as a *bid* and turn toward it. Always. If you did nothing else, this one discipline would completely transform your relationship. You would grow continually closer to her, you'd get to know her more and more deeply, and she would turn toward *your* bids more and more.

She could say, "It pisses me off when you seem to be so casual with our money, when I try so hard to save money." *That is a bid for connection.* She is telling you what she values and asking you to join her in those values.

The best way to get in the habit of turning toward all her bids is to make limited-in-time commitments to practice the discipline. So, for example, make a decision on your next day off with her to do your very best — focusing on it all day — to turn toward every single one of her bids for connection.

Then some other day, do the same thing. Focus on just *that* all day. This will make you very aware of bids and your responses. Over time this will change the way you respond to her bids, and that will change your relationship for the better. Both of you will be happier.

Capitalizing

Shelly Gable, an assistant professor of psychology at UCLA who studies what makes marriages great, has found something helpful. It's really a variation on this idea of turning toward bids.

Her research discovered that when a husband or wife tells some good news to their spouse, the spouse's reaction can *raise* the husband's or wife's mood, or *lower* it, and the response has longer-term consequences too.

If your woman tells you some good news, how do you typically respond? Gable divided the possible kinds of responses into four categories.

For example, if your woman told you she just got a promotion at work, you might respond in one of these four ways:

1. **Enthusiastically:** "That's great, Honey! You earned it!"

2. **Negatively or critically:** "Are they going to make you work longer hours?"

3. **Positive, but subdued:** "That's nice."

4. **Uninterested:** "Did you see they finally opened the new Macy's on 8th Street?"

Studies show that when you respond enthusiastically (known as "capitalizing"), as opposed to any of the other ways, it makes a big difference in how satisfied your wife is in your relationship, how committed she is, and how in love with you she is.

And, of course, if your woman is more satisfied with your relationship, more committed to you, and more in love with you, *you* will be happier too!

This is something relatively simple you can do that will produce a lot of benefits. When I first read about this study, I immediately realized that my wife (Klassy Evans) responds enthusiastically *every* time something good happens to me or for me. And what do you know? I feel totally committed to her, completely satisfied with my marriage, and deeply in love with her.

And on the heels of that realization, I also recognized that I wasn't doing that for her. I never even *thought* about it. Sometimes I responded enthusiastically, sometimes positively but subdued, sometimes even negatively or uninterested. I couldn't believe it.

But it was an easy thing to remedy. I immediately started looking for even the smallest bit of good news she told me, and I now make sure I give her the enthusiasm she deserves.

You can see that Gable's studies dovetail with Gottman's notion of bids. Responding enthusiastically or "positively but subdued" are both "turning toward." Responding negatively is the same as Gottman's "turning against." And Gable's "uninterested" is similar to Gottman's "turning away."

All this research supports the idea that both of you will be happier in your relationship if you turn *toward* all her bids for connection. And you can prove it to yourself. Make a concentrated effort to turn toward *all* her bids for connection, big and small, and watch what happens. It will change your life.

Perfection

As I said earlier, I'm not *great* at putting any of these ideas into practice. I'm always getting better, but I'm not good at it. And it doesn't really matter. If I turn toward her bids one out of five times, that is *way* better than one in ten, and infinitely better than never.

Don't get upset with yourself or think less of yourself when you forget or don't do it well. You're a man. You have strengths and weaknesses, and sometimes your strengths in one area make you weak in another. That's the way it is. Just do your best and consider every time you turn toward a bid of hers as a triumph, a victory, and a win.

The same is true for the other ideas in this book. Don't expect yourself to ever master them. Relationships and connection are not your genetic domain. You are out of your element, especially compared with her, so cut yourself some slack. But every move you make in the right direction makes things better. Focus on what you do well, focus on your good choices, and don't dwell on your mistakes.

It would be a mistake to put too much attention on your mistakes. Men don't learn well that way. As Ralph Waldo Emerson wrote, "Do not be too timid and squeamish about your actions. All life is an experiment."

Experiments

Nothing can teach you better than first-hand experience. Information is great, but personal experience can teach lessons you will never forget. So I've got some experiments for you to try.

Let's start with bids. For one week or even one *day*, make up your mind that you will turn toward *all* her bids. Turn *toward*, not against or away. This will show you a) it's not as easy as it sounds, and b) what a huge difference it could make if you did it more often.

If she makes a bid and you can see no way to turn toward it, *write it down*. Later take the time to brainstorm ways you could turn toward that kind of bid next time.

Set a target. One day. Two days. A week. Whatever you think you can do, and make it specific. And then don't concentrate on anything else with her except that. See everything she says to you as a bid for connection and turn toward them all.

Even if she starts humming a tune, *turn toward it* — hum along with her or give her a backbeat or hug her and tell her you like the way she sounds.

If she asks you if you want something at the store because she is going to stop by there on the way home, *thank her for asking.*

If she gives you a dirty look, ask her, "What?" Even her dirty look is a bid for connection. She is offering emotional information. You can turn toward it, turn away from it, or turn against it. Turn *toward* it. Tell her you want to know all about what she is feeling right now. Stop avoiding her negativity. You'll find out why in the next chapter.

Write the principle on a card and carry it with you for the period of time you've decided on to constantly remind you, because you will keep forgetting.

This is an *experiment*. Turn toward all her bids for a set period of time and pay attention to what happens. Do you like the end result?

Take Her Suggestions

John Gottman says if he could sum up all his findings into one sentence, it would simply be: *A marriage does better if the man accepts influence from his wife.*

I have greatly benefited from Klassy's influence, and that's an understatement if I've ever made one! I have done this experiment many times, and every time I do, it is illuminating. The experiment is to take *every* suggestion she makes for a week, or even just one day.

If she suggests something, just do it, without even considering it. Don't tell her you're doing this experiment until after it's over. Just easily, without any fan-fare, take every suggestion from her, every recommendation she gives you, as wise counsel from the Oracle, and do it.

When I do this, I find that the things she suggests are always in my best interest. And doing this exercise makes me acutely aware that I must normally disregard many of her suggestions. But that is foolish of me and counterproductive, especially to disregard any suggestions she has about relationships.

When you two talk about something *you* are good at or know a lot about, *you* are the authority. But when you talk about relationships, connection, communication, *she* is the authority, and you should defer to her opinion.

And the same goes with integrity. If she is talking about something having to do with "doing the right thing," she is the authority, and you would be wise to take her suggestions.

Do you know that in developing countries, studies have been done on what people do when they get a little money? Very poor people in those countries often subsist by growing crops. And researchers have found that men tend to grow crops they can *sell*, while women tend to grow *food* their own children can eat.

And the researchers found another difference between the sexes. When it is a particularly good growing season and they have a little surplus, after the men sell their crops, they have a greater tendency to spend their surplus money on alcohol, tobacco and prostitutes.

The women, when they have a choice, tend to spend surplus money on food and schooling for their children (in developing countries, parents often have to *pay* for schooling for their children, and school isn't required by law).

This is a demonstration of women's innate goodness and integrity. By and large, women are more likely to act with integrity than men. And men are better off if they allow women to influence them. It makes for a more wholesome life.

From the time Ulysses S. Grant first met Julia, he was devoted to her. Everyone who knew Grant before and after he met Julia could see what a difference she made in his life. A friend of his commented that Grant was "overly attached to his wife." Another said, "He came out of his shell in her presence."

The historian, Mark Perry, wrote that Grant's loyalty to Julia was "lavishly repaid. Through all the years ahead, including those that were the most difficult of his life, Julia never lost confidence in her husband's abilities, always believed in his greatness, and remained unerringly loyal."

When Grant was just a young officer, long before the Civil War, he was once sent away to Corpus Christi during the war with Mexico in the late 1840s. He missed his wife, Julia, and wrote to her, "In going away now I feel as if I had someone else than myself to live and strive to do well for. You can have but little idea of the influence you have over me Julia, even while so far away. If I feel tempted to do any thing that I think is not right I am sure to think, 'Well now if Julia saw me would I do so' and thus it is absent or present I am more or less governed by what I think is your will."

During the Civil War, Grant rose through the ranks until he became the top general in the Union Army. In fact, he was granted a rank that nobody had been given since George Washington.

And after the war, he was elected to two terms as President. Being guided and influenced by his wife obviously did not reduce his manliness or his ability to succeed in the world. I think he would have said the influence of his wife *helped* him succeed throughout his life.

The same is likely true for you. If you accept more of her influence, your relationships will probably improve (because she knows more about connection) but your success in the world is likely to benefit too.

Ask Her For Advice

Men are notorious for not wanting to ask for advice. But it is not impossible to do, and when you do it, I think you'll be pleasantly surprised at the quality of the advice your woman gives you.

Because of her different strengths, her point of view can be very different from yours, giving you a new look at your situation. You don't have to *take* her advice. But if nothing else, it can widen your view.

Think about some problem you are having. Just one. Or think of something that has been challenging for you. When you come up with a good one, sometime today say, "I want your advice about something." And then tell her as much detail as you can about the problem or situation. And ask, "What do you think I should do about it?"

Discuss it All

Here's another, somewhat related, experiment: Run every decision by her for one week. *Every* decision, big or small, except of course what you have to make on the fly when she's not there. But try to talk to her about *every single decision* you make for some set period of time.

Men are quicker to make decisions, and are capable of acting with more decisiveness, but we are also more prone to making *bad* decisions because those decisions were made hastily.

When you think about running everything by her, isn't your first reaction, "No, I don't want to do that because she'll want to discuss it in painful detail?" So normally, in order to avoid the misery and tedium of talking about things at such great length, you just make the decision on your own.

But consider for a moment what that "says" to her. By not talking to her, especially about things that affect her, you have taken the position of boss. By not discussing it with her and by deciding *for* her, you've overridden her equal authority because you don't like the way she does things. So you have, even if you did not "mean" to, controlled her. You have dominated her.

Especially if the outcome of the decision affects her, as an experiment, try discussing it with her. You'll be surprised that often in the discussions, she comes up with things you hadn't thought of — things you care about, things you're *glad* she brought to your attention because they change your decision.

Sometimes it will feel as if she slows things down. You want to just make a decision and get into action. She wants to talk about it and think about it. You want the discussion to conclude and a decision to be made. She is less driven to act, and perfectly willing to not come to a conclusion today but to just ruminate about it for a few days. What is the big urgency? From her point of view, there is no reason it has to be decided now. But she doesn't have a brain and body driving her to *move forward* with the same kind of inner urgency you feel.

But for the experiment, just go along with her desire to discuss it. Offer your thoughts. Say what you know. Say what you think. Say what you want. Find out more if that seems appropriate. Take longer if she wants to. Feel free to offer possible decisions, but come to the decisions *together*, and if she doesn't want to decide yet, yield to that.

This is an experiment, so pay attention to the quality of the decisions, the amount of time they took, and see if this policy might be something you want to use more often.

List of Appreciation

Sit down and make a list of all the things about her you appreciate. This will take awhile. After you've made your initial list, keep thinking about it over the next few days, and add to the list as you think of more. And when you're done, give her a copy. But also keep a copy and read it yourself once in awhile.

And notice how this changes *you*. Like the rest of the human race, you have a tendency to take good things for granted. But just because that's a natural tendency doesn't mean you're stuck with it. At any given moment, you can remember what you appreciate about her, and when you do, it'll change your attitude toward her.

The mind has a negative bias in some ways. It tends to fixate on what is wrong and overlook what is right. It's worth the trouble to rise above this tendency, at least once in awhile. It will make you both happier if you do. Those who make the small effort required to think about what they're grateful for, even for brief moments (but every day) are measurably happier.

According to the research, your woman's outstanding traits are what probably originally attracted you to her, but now they annoy you. The outstanding traits you found *most* endearing about her are traits you now find the *most* irritating about her.

Why is this? Because those traits are *outstanding*. They stand out. She embodies those characteristics more than most people do.

When I read this study, I thought about what I would consider an "annoying trait" of Klassy's. It was an easy question to answer. It is her stubbornness, her unwillingness to just "go along," her unwillingness to be dominated or controlled. This seems especially infuriating when I'm angry.

Then I thought about what first attracted me to her. This was also an easy question to answer. It was her courage, her psychological strength, her absolute clarity about what she wants and feels, her ability to resist peer pressure. I was so impressed with her clear-eyed, brave, open-hearted personal power.

It's the same trait!

Think about what it is for your woman, and make sure that trait is on your list of what you appreciate. And hopefully from now on, when you would normally have been annoyed by that trait, you will see it in a new light, and appreciate it.

While people are not usually appreciative of what blessings they have, with a very small amount of effort, we can enjoy more gratitude, and when we do, it not only benefits us, it benefits those closest to us too. Make your list and find out for yourself.

Five Acknowledgments a Day

Another way to work around the fact that you tend to take good things for granted is to acknowledge what you like. *Say* it. Try this experiment: For the next week, give your woman five acknowledgments a day.

It's okay if she knows you're doing this experiment. She would probably figure out you were up to something anyway.

A good acknowledgment will be specific and will explain *why* you liked it. Say specifically what she did that you liked rather than saying something more general like "You're great." Here are some examples:

Thanks for mailing that box for me, honey. I really wanted it done, but I didn't have time to go to the post office.

Thank you for being honest with me yesterday when you told me you didn't want to go to the park. I really like it that you don't make me guess what you want.

This afternoon, I know you really wanted me to get up, but you let me sleep anyway. Thank you so much. I needed that nap and feel much better.

Acknowledge what you want more of. Give it attention. Acknowledge things you have taken for granted. Acknowledge what you're grateful for.

And acknowledge what you see about her that perhaps she hasn't been able to acknowledge in herself. That kind of acknowledgment is not just nice. It can change her life. An acknowledgment Klassy gave me did that for me.

When I was a teenager, I had a private fantasy that I would be a writer some day. But nobody knew about it and nobody ever told me I was a good writer. Flash forward to being married to Klassy. I had written something and she wrote me a note in a card. On the card was a photograph of a beautiful rock formation in Arizona. She wrote, "There are few great things in this world. Your writing is one of them."

It was the first time anyone had acknowledged me as a writer, and it was such a powerful acknowledgment because it validated something in me I *hoped* was true. That's the kind of acknowledgment that can change someone's life. It changed mine. It changed the whole trajectory of my life.

This wasn't the only time she acknowledged me and encouraged me to do something that I hadn't found the courage to pursue myself.

So look at your woman with this in mind: Is there something she secretly hopes she has the talent for, but for which the world has given her no notice? Is there something inside her aching to get out, but needs some encouragement or validation from the outside world? If you find something like that, give the best acknowledgement you can. Your attention will be like water to a wilting plant. You will see her blossom.

When you do this experiment and give five good acknowledgments a day, you will find that it causes more changes than you think it would. You normally have your attention on certain things. But when you're in the midst of this experiment, your attention will continually return to thinking about something you can acknowledge — something you want more of, something you like about her, and having your mind on such things is very pleasant.

This shift of your attention not only makes *her* feel more appreciated, it makes *your* life more enjoyable. Try it and you'll see what I mean.

Balance Criticism With the Whole Truth

Sometimes you may feel the need to criticize her. When you do, if it makes her feel bad, tell her the rest of the truth: "That does not nullify the fact that I love you, I care about you, and I really appreciate all you do for me." Or say whatever positive truth you can think of.

Balancing your criticism like that will help both of you. It'll keep you freshly aware of the positive truths, soften the sharpness of your criticisms, and reduce the sting.

Take Her Point of View

This is one of the most interesting and illuminating experiments you can make. Imagine seeing out of her eyes. Sit down and close your eyes and relax your body for a minute. Then imagine a recent conversation you two had. In your imagination, float up out of your own body, and float down into her body and look at *you* from her eyes. Listen to *you* with her ears.

Just stay there looking out from her eyes for a little while as the conversation continues. You'll get a whole new perspective. Literally.

You look different from her point of view than you do from your own. You sound different. Try it and you'll find out for yourself. And afterward you will probably treat her differently — in a good way.

Another way to help you empathize with her point of view is to read fiction. According to research, reading fiction will improve your empathy, not just for her, but for other people. Reading fiction has been shown to improve the reader's ability to see things from another's point of view, to be more open to new experiences, and to become more socially aware. That's a lot of benefit for something that's actually enjoyable to do.

Fiction gets its effect from your emotional connection to the characters in the story and from temporarily setting aside your own point of view and goals and taking on the point of view and goals of the protagonist. So it functions like "point of view training." We don't normally get outside our own point of view. But it is something that naturally happens when you read a good fiction story. I haven't seen any studies about reading memoirs, but I would guess the same would be true for non-fiction memoirs, and for the same reason.

But however you do it, try to see you and your relationship from *her* point of view, and the best, most direct way to do that is to literally imagine what things look like from her eyes.

Do this once in awhile, especially at times when you've been in an argument and you don't understand why she reacted the way she did.

Speak With "Excessive" Accuracy

One of the differences in the way men and women communicate is that she uses more qualifiers and expresses less certainty than you do when she talks. A man might say, for example, "They all do that." A woman would say, "I sometimes think almost all of them do that. Don't you?"

The difference can be subtle, but it has consequences. Her statement is probably more accurate, but less persuasive. One of the side-effects of testosterone is excessive (unjustified by the facts) confidence. And that includes confidence in what you think and say. Men have a tendency to be less accurate than women, but feel more confident about it.

This has some benefits but can also have some negative consequences. It's beneficial when you're trying to convince another. They can be fooled by the confidence with which you speak, and so get the false impression that you know what you're talking about. If you happen to be right, this is a good thing. If you happen to be wrong, however, you just added more confusion and misinformation into the world — something we definitely don't need any more of. And your listener will trust you less.

In your personal relationships, this kind of overconfidence is damaging in the same way lying is damaging. You are, in effect, *lying* when you state something with too much certainty and too few qualifications than is justified by what you know. You're *misleading* her. The closer you can get to accuracy and honesty with her, the better your relationship will be. You become more trustworthy, so she gains trust in you, which gives her feelings of security and safety (in other words, releases oxytocin into her system).

So try this experiment, just for training purposes, just for the purpose of generating insight. For a pre-determined period of time, make an effort to be more accurate with your speech. Add qualifiers where they're needed to make more accurate statements. Only *act* confident when you really and truly know *for sure* that what you're saying is true (which won't be very often).

The reason I'm calling these *experiments* is that you don't have to do them all the time. All these experiments are good things to do in general, but it would be exhausting to try to do them every day. But doing one for a set period can really improve your awareness of it, and teach you its value without committing yourself to the burden of constant effort.

And if you keep experimenting, you will eventually adopt some of these experimental ideas as your usual way of being, and that will benefit your relationship.

Use Comparisons to Your Advantage

Your mind can be justifiably seen as a comparison-making machine. You compare all the time without even trying. You compare your life to other peoples' lives. You compare *your* level of success to others'. And you compare your woman to other women.

Although you will often naturally notice that your woman is superior to others, it's also true that the human brain is biased toward the negative in many ways, and the structure of reality often gives you a negatively biased perception of reality, so your comparisons will often make you feel worse. You'll compare your life and your woman to what you don't have and what you'd like, and you'll compare your woman as she is in the privacy of your home with women all dressed up in public, on their best behavior, or airbrushed in magazines.

And while that may be the most natural, automatic way your brain makes comparisons, *you're not stuck with it.* You can make comparisons on purpose. You can make comparisons that serve you, make you happier, and improve your relationship. And you can do it deliberately.

As an experiment, just for a day, deliberately compare your woman to women you know who are worse than your woman in some way. If you know a woman who is a real bitch, compare her with your woman and feel how glad you are that your woman is not like that. If your woman has particularly nice skin, compare that to other women who don't have such nice skin.

This is a way to feel grateful, to count your blessings. It is perfectly natural to take what you have for granted, and to keep your attention focused on what you *don't* have. The grass is always greener. But this natural way of using your attention isn't good for you or your relationship. And it is simply not true. You chose your woman for good reason. It will make you two happier together if you at least occasionally notice those things you normally take for granted that you appreciate. This experiment is one way to do that.

Another way to do it is to simply ponder the question, "About her, what am I grateful for?" Just think about this for the day, as you go on about your business.

Watch Don Juan

Watch the version of the movie starring Faye Dunaway, Marlon Brando, and Johnny Depp. You will see a great demonstration of a man who shifts his values to love. And you'll see a demonstration of a man who begins to pour his attention and appreciation on his woman, and how she blooms.

You should watch this movie once a year, just to keep yourself aware of the value of love. Brando plays a successful man who has been married a long time. He takes his woman for granted. She loves him and looks out for him, but the spark has gone out of their marriage and they've both accepted it as an inevitable part of life.

But Brando is an accomplished psychiatrist who is treating an unusual patient, a young man who believes himself to be Don Juan, and he challenges Brando to look at his relationship in a new way, and Brando does. He starts paying attention to his wife for the first time in a long time. You can see that for her, *finally* her life is what she has always thought it could be. At long last, love is at the center of their lives, where it should be, and she's happy. They're both happy.

Watch the movie, and use it as a metaphor for your own life. Use it as a seminar on how to be happy.

Use Her Criticisms

Take her complaints and criticisms as something you could use. Find a way they can be useful to you personally and selfishly. Try to find some way to think, "I am glad she said that," and mean it.

For example, let's say she tells you, "There's always an excuse. You never take responsibility." That kind of statement, can, of course, hurt your feelings, and the first thing you want to do is say how that is completely unfair or inaccurate. But what would happen if you tried to *use* it? What if you took that criticism as useful information? What if you considered that you had organized a team of experts on psychology or success and they had done a battery of tests on you, and that was their conclusion? What kind of solutions might they offer?

What if they told you that if you could take care of that particular fault of yours, you could be considerably happier and more successful? What would you do?

At the very least, you would *think* about it, right? You would consider it. You'd try to figure out what you could do about it. You'd look into different areas of your life to decide how you might be sabotaging your own success by neglecting to take responsibility or making excuses.

So do that with her criticisms. She probably knows you at least as well as a team of psychologists and success experts after a series of tests, and she cares about you and wants you to be happy. And besides, it is likely that if you are doing something counterproductive with her, it's probably something you do with other people too, but others may not be willing to speak as honestly with you as your woman does, so you may be shooting yourself in the foot without realizing it. Her "complaint" is an opportunity for you to make your life better, but only if you take it that way.

So just as an experiment, pick a day and take every criticism she makes as the most brilliant and useful insight you could have from any source. Write down what she says and ponder how the insight could make your whole life better.

Watch the Dog Whisperer

Learn what it means to be assertive but calm and loving. Cesar Millan, the Dog Whisperer, demonstrates it continually. He is not a wimp with the dogs, but he is not overly dominant. He is a leader, but not a tyrant. He asserts what he wants, but he allows the dogs to be what they are.

Watch Cesar at work and really grasp the principle and see it in action in many different circumstances and contexts. *Study* it.

It may seem that you can *either* be assertive *or* calm. But it is entirely possible to be both simultaneously. It is not only possible, it is ideal.

When you achieve this state, she will love it and so will you.

Assume You Don't Know

Some of what you believe would make her happy is mistaken. And some of what you don't think would make her happy would, actually, make her happy.

You're a human being, so you don't perceive the world perfectly. You see through the filter of your own biases and prejudice, influenced by your male brain and your male hormones.

So for an experiment, for one whole day, *assume you don't know*. Assume that everything you think you know might be mistaken, and try to find out from her.

Notice, ask, pay attention, listen carefully, watch carefully. What does she really care about? What does she want from you? And what *doesn't* she seem to care about?

Not only is it likely that you have mistakenly assumed many things about her, but you have also probably misunderstood things about her, and on top of all that, she has changed her mind about some things and you haven't updated what you think you know about her. You have to have an open mind to update what you believe to be true about her. Assuming you don't know is a good way to open your mind.

Notice What You Haven't Noticed

Assume there are things your woman does for you that you have failed to notice, and see if you can discover what they are. And then acknowledge them. Tell her you (finally) noticed and thank her for doing them for you.

You know how sometimes when you're driving, you have the experience of not really paying attention for awhile? You may even miss your turnoff because you were "spacing out." Ellen Langer, a researcher who studies "mindlessness" says these moments happen more often than we think. We're not really here, not really noticing. And, of course, many times we don't notice that we're not noticing.

Her suggestion for overcoming this human tendency is to nurture a new habit — to notice something new about your environment or the person you're talking with. *Notice something new.* Try to find something you've never noticed before. Langer has been doing groundbreaking research on mindlessness for *decades.* We should take her advice.

Trying to notice something you've never noticed before brings you into the present moment. And for our purposes, it can help you become aware of things your woman does for you, services she provides for you, actions she takes on your behalf that you've taken for granted or have never even known about.

That's your mission. Find out what she's doing for you that you haven't noticed, and thank her for it.

Build Your Riches

Every experience you've ever had in your life made a series of pathways in your brain. It's a pattern of connections between brain cells. Recalling an experience *reinforces* the pathways, making the memory stronger, more vivid and easier to recall in the future. If you never think about an event again, the memory fades.

In a way, our memories are our only true riches. We can choose to strengthen the good memories or we can neglect them, let them fade, and it will feel to us as if not much good has ever happened.

The best way to strengthen a memory is to reminisce, of course. So here is the experiment: Sit down with her and play a game; take turns coming up with a happy memory of an experience you had together, and whoever is coming up with the memory tries to come up with details about the experience the other had forgotten or never knew.

You come up with one, talk about it for awhile, and then she comes up with one. Go back and forth, take your time. Enjoy the process. You're making your good memories unforgettable. You are building your true riches.

Ask Her For a Mission

You are driven to take action. You want to make her happy. But you don't understand her and really don't like to stop and discuss things or take the time to think things through. You don't like to weigh all the options. You want to get *moving*. You want to *do* something. But often what you do is something you wish you hadn't done.

But she has all the strengths you're missing. So just ask her to tell you how you can be her action hero. Ask her for a mission. Even a small one. It will help make you both happy.

At first she may not have anything for you. She may not be able to think of anything quickly, and she may not feel right about giving you something to do. But keep asking her now and then. It will get her mind pondering the possibility and it will allow her to become more comfortable with the idea. Eventually she will think of something.

For this experiment, take a day, a weekend, or an entire week and ask her a couple of times a day if she can think of a mission for you — something you can carry out for her, some action you can take for her — and be ready to carry out that mission when she comes up with one.

The time you most want an action to take is when she's upset. You want to make things right. You want her to stop being upset. At times like that, you can ask her for a mission, but if she can't think of anything on the spot, let it go. More on that in the next chapter.

She is Happy
When You're Upset

The title of this chapter is just a catchy headline. She doesn't really want you to be upset. But that's how it feels sometimes, doesn't it? And it isn't terribly far from the truth.

Men sometimes feel that their women start arguments only in order to have an argument. And doesn't it feel sometimes like your woman isn't satisfied until *you* get upset? Have you ever felt that way?

Researchers looked into this, and what they found can change your life. In an experiment with a mix of 156 married and unmarried couples, they videoed each couple talking about a recent upsetting incident they'd had.

Then the researchers had each couple watch their own video while they were questioned about how each of them felt at different points during the conversation on the video.

What they found is intriguing and has significant implications for you and your marriage. Men didn't like it when the conversation was upsetting. Men were happiest when their women were happy, or at least in a good mood. They wanted *pleasantness*.

The women, on the other hand, were happiest when the men were upset. That's when the women felt most connected in the conversation — when their man was "distressed," or when the man realized that his woman was suffering.

Now, from a man's perspective, that sounds like a criticism of women, as if they are negative or even cruel torturers, but it reveals something fundamentally different between the sexes that is very important for you to understand.

What you want is *pleasantness* between you and your woman. You want her to be in a good mood, you want the two of you to be happy together. She wants that too, but she values something else even more — honesty. She wants to know how you *really* feel. She wants to know what you *really* think. And she wants that far more than she wants pleasantness. Far *far* more. She values pleasantness very little. And she values dishonest or misleading pleasantness not at all.

If you two are married, or if she considers it a real possibility that you two will be married some day, or if you will be for all intents and purposes married by common law, then she is tied to you financially and emotionally. And you are more active and aggressive than she is. You're physically bigger than she is. You have a harder time sharing what you really feel about things because of the structure of your brain and the influence of testosterone. You're less likely to realize love is the most important thing in life. And you are likely to be less committed to open communication and honesty.

Because of all this, she feels vulnerable. Because of all this, she *is* vulnerable.

So she feels most reassured when she *knows* you're being honest with her. That is when she feels the most secure — when she *knows* you are telling her the truth. She wants to be able to *count* on you, which requires authenticity and honesty.

You are bigger, more aggressive, more prone to action, less perceptive, more confident, and you take more action. With someone like you, pleasantness is *dangerous*. Pleasantness probably means some information is being hidden, because let's face it, reality is not always pleasant.

If you were going to guess if a friend of yours was being honest with you, which would you guess is a more honest expression? When he is smiling and letting you know everything is just fine? Or when he is visibly upset about something and telling you about it?

Obviously, you would guess he is most likely being honest when he's upset. That would be the way to bet.

Women make the same obvious calculation. So it's not that your woman wants you to be upset and feel bad. It's that your woman wants most desperately to really know you, to feel close to you, to be intimate with you, and the most sure way of making that happen is to encourage you to speak your mind when you are upset. And she will feel most reassured that the honest truth is being told when you are visibly upset.

Beyond that, a man who doesn't really care much about a relationship or who isn't "engaged" in it is far more likely to be pleasant and make sure everything seems "just fine." Someone who is truly serious about his relationship is more likely to at least occasionally speak seriously and be upset. A man who really wants his woman to truly know him and who wants to really know his woman will be serious and upset more often. That's one of the prices you will have to be willing to pay in order to have a good, close, loving, caring, honest, committed connection with your woman.

What should you do with this information? Feign upset once in awhile so your woman is happy? No, that would completely miss the point.

What you should do is remember this and realize that you have a tendency to want everything to be nice. You have a tendency to avoid conflict and upsets, even if you have to avoid talking about things with her. Just realize you will want that, and occasionally or more often *speak your mind anyway*, engage in a real conversation, be honest, and be willing for it to be unpleasant in the service of connection and intimacy.

You will both be happier in the long run if you do this. You will have a real connection, not a superficial *show* of pleasantness with unknown issues lurking underneath. You will also have a woman who feels more secure in her relationship.

How to Deal With Arguments

When you're in an argument with your mate, you are out of your element. Your body reacts like you're in physical combat, as if lives are at stake and strenuous action needs to be taken if those lives are to be saved.

Your body is reacting as if it is living in another time. It's like a machine that was built for the defense of a family in a wild world — defense against large predators, and defense against hostile warriors.

Your body is evolved perfectly for this task. Its blood coagulates quickly, closing up wounds and preventing the loss of blood; there are excessive red blood cells per drop to carry oxygen quickly to muscles; the adrenaline system reacts quickly to activate the body at a moment's notice; the brain reacts to adrenaline quickly to shift blood flow to the motor cortex, so your movements can be as precise and coordinated as possible; your eyes are designed for excellent depth perception so you can strike a blow against the predators or warriors and make sure your blow lands in the right place on the first try.

Your body is like an exquisitely designed hunting warrior machine — perfectly equipped to deal with battling and big game hunting.

But it has gone through a kind of time-machine, so to speak, and sent into the future. And what it must deal with now is something entirely different than it was built for — a completely non-physical verbal argument with a woman — a woman who has a body and brain built for just such a task.

You are outmatched. You are not in your element. This is a difficult situation, and requires you to do a few things to compensate — things that might not feel natural, especially at first.

But luckily, the best superiority human beings have over all other animals is our ability to learn to do things that don't come naturally.

You can't avoid arguments with your mate. They are inevitable. You *will* argue. There *will* be times when you are angry with each other. Even though in *your* mind an argument with her is more dangerous to *her* because your blood pressure goes up more, because your brain switches to "physical action" mode, because you have a greater tendency to want to dominate her, and because you are physically more suited to combat, you would think *she* would try harder than *you* to avoid arguments, but as you well know, that is not the case. It doesn't make *any* sense at all from a man's point of view.

You want to *avoid* upsetting conversations. She doesn't seem to have your sense of aversion. You feel it is dangerous. Your heart pounds, you want to punch a hole in the wall. You feel it creates a volatile, dangerous situation, you don't know what you might do if you got too upset, so you want to stop the fight before something bad happens.

But you also want to get your point across and it seems like she is being deliberately dense or stubborn. It's an infuriating situation. What should be done during times like these?

I want you to remember something; a principle, a truth: You can't avoid conflict if you're in a committed relationship, you cannot avoid arguments, but you *can* avoid *escalation*.

Think of an argument as a negative feedback loop. It's similar to putting a microphone near a speaker. If the two get close enough, and if the volume is loud enough, you'll have the possibility of the sound going into the microphone and coming out the speaker loudly enough that the microphone will pick up *that* sound and amplify it and put it through the speaker again, which will come out even *louder*, which will be picked up by the mic and put through the speaker again even louder, etc.

It'll get louder and louder until something breaks.

An argument is like that. The upset escalates, at least sometimes. Your upsetting feelings put certain looks on your face, put certain tones in your voice, cause you to say harsh things, and all this elevates *her* level of upset, which does the same to her, and when you see her and hear her getting madder and meaner, it makes you even *more* mad, etc. You're in a negative feedback loop and it's *escalating*.

What should you do? The same thing you would do with the microphone and speaker — separate them. If you can get that microphone away from the speaker, the escalation will stop. The feedback loop is stopped.

If you can get yourself away from the argument, the same will happen. It is sometimes perplexing how *quickly* it happens. I've been in an argument with Klassy and stormed out of the house to go for a walk, slamming the door behind me, and within six steps, I already regret what I just said. In the heat of the moment, in the midst of the anger, I am essentially insane. You too.

John Gottman has discovered that when your heart rate is over a hundred beats per minute, you stop being reasonable. When you're upset enough that your heart is racing, any conversation with you is going to be pointless. You are no longer rational. You can no longer be reasoned with. It is not likely to be a productive conversation. Very few problems are going to get solved. The only thing likely to happen is feelings are going to get hurt.

And a hundred beats per minute isn't very high. I have tested my heart rate during an upset, at a time when I was what I considered only "mildly upset," and my heart rate was about a hundred and twenty. I have yet to be sane enough when I was *really* upset to test my heart rate.

When you feel an upsetting argument beginning to escalate, *take a break*. Go do something else. Gottman says it takes about twenty minutes for your body to calm down again enough to talk reasonably. I have tested these rules of thumb repeatedly and they are good. Remember these numbers: At over a hundred beats per minute, it's time to stop talking and leave the room until you calm down. And give yourself twenty minutes to calm down.

I know I just said earlier that she is happiest when you are upset, but that means only *mildly* upset. It means you are dealing with what may be an unpleasant issue to talk about, and the two of you perhaps *slightly* raise your voice or display some other signs of upset.

But when you're raising your voice and can't seem to tone it down, and it's starting to get very upsetting, take a break. I think you will find that this is difficult. Hopefully your woman will help you out with this. When you're mad, you *really* want to get your point across. You don't want to stop. If she ever asks you to stop and take a break, *please stop.* And do your best to stop on your own when you feel the intensity get too high. Good luck with it. I have done it successfully many times, but usually Klassy is the one to stop me. She and I know about Gottman's research, and she just says, "I think we should take a break." Usually she has to tell me a few times before I take her advice.

How do you know when you are too upset and should probably take a break if you don't take your pulse to find out? Here's another good rule of thumb: A good time to take a break is when *she* seems unreasonable.

When *you* are no longer reasonable, *she* will seem no longer reasonable, whether she is or not. And because of the phenomenon of the negative feedback loop, if you are upset enough to raise your heart rate enough to be unreasonable, it is likely that hers has raised enough to be unreasonable too. But you will not notice that *you* have lost your reason. The first thing you'll notice is that *she* has lost her sanity. She no longer makes sense. It seems to you she is being stupid, or deliberately hard-headed, or she has lost her mind. From now on, that means it's time to stop talking to each other.

Go for a walk or watch a video or go into another room and surf the internet. Whatever. Do not stay in the same room with her. Let your body calm back down. And don't just go into another room and *fume*. Do something to *get your mind off it* for twenty minutes.

Once you have calmed down, if you still want to talk about it, you can try again.

One of the most curious things about doing this is that sometimes, after you have calmed down, there doesn't seem to be anything you need to talk about. You were simply temporarily obsessed by something that doesn't really matter.

Solving Problems by Avoiding Them

I almost called this "The perplexing phenomenon of problems that disappear because we don't talk about them." Over and over it happens. She tells me she doesn't want to talk to me when I'm angry. But I really, *strongly* want to talk about it right then.

But eventually if she doesn't want to talk to me, I go do something else for awhile. And once I've calmed down, there doesn't seem to be a problem. Sometimes I have a hard time remembering what only a short while ago seemed like a vitally important thing she *had* to know. Have you ever had this experience? How is it possible?

The feedback loop has sent you into a different state of mind, and in that state of mind, you're literally not sane. So things that seem vitally important to you when you're raging mad don't seem important at all when you're in your "right mind." And other things that are normally very important to you (like her happiness) become very unimportant to you when you are raging mad.

So you may be extremely intent on getting some point across when you're angry, and you don't want to stop talking about it and take a break because she *needs* to get this point, she *must* get this point and agree with you, even if it kills you, but then after calming down, and you are ready to talk about it, there doesn't really seem to be a problem. You just needed to say something very simple, so you say it, and there's no problem, no upset, no nothing.

So in a sense, you solved the problem by deliberately not talking about it.

Of course, there are plenty of problems that need to be talked about and solved and will not disappear when you avoid talking about them. But they will feel like problems even when you're not upset.

Okay, let me summarize. This is a great truth that was hard won: When your heart rate goes over a hundred, the chances of the argument escalating start going up. And the chances of the argument turning into something hurtful and ugly, something that will take days to get over, and that can potentially cause hurt you can never get over, keep going up.

But the chances of things getting worse by taking a break are almost nonexistent.

If you stay in the argument as it escalates, you have a greater and greater chance of saying or doing something you'll regret.

But if you take a break, the chances that you'll do something you regret are slim.

Logically then — mathematically — it would make the most sense to take a break and simmer down. Of course, you're not reasonable at the time this break needs to be taken, so how are you going to have the sense to take a break?

If I was you, I would enlist her to help you. Talk to her about this chapter and ask her to refuse to talk to you when you seem unreasonable. You can even ask her to insist that you check your heart rate and not talk to you until it gets below a hundred. Klassy and I have done that and it works very well. We use one of those automatic blood pressure monitors — it measures the heart rate too.

If You Have a Hot Temper

If you just get too upset during arguments, start a regular practice of mantra meditation. It's easy to do. On adamlikhan.com, we have instructions for how to meditate, but probably the best way to learn to meditate is by listening to recorded instructions. I recommend the meditation instructions by Shinzen Young or Patricia Carrington.

Meditation alters your physiology, making you less reactive. In studies of people who meditate regularly, researchers found that meditators don't get as upset as non-meditators. When shown disturbing images, for example — the kind of images that normally produce a stress reaction in people — meditators' heart rates didn't rise as much as non-meditators, and those heart rates returned to normal faster.

These are useful changes if you happen to be very reactive normally. Meditation has many other positive benefits. But if you seem to get too angry too quickly and you'd like to slow down your reaction time, meditate. It's been shown to have a measurably calming effect at even fifteen minutes a day. If you have a problem with a short temper, cutting out caffeine would help too.

Be There

One thing you can do to help avoid escalating arguments in the first place is learn to listen without *doing* anything. Learn to just be there and experience unpleasant feelings and hear her describing her unpleasant feelings, and just *be* there.

You're a man, so you have a desire to take action, to solve the problem, to fix things. So when she is describing a problem to you, that is your first impulse. You want to make a decision and get into action. But often this is not what she is looking for.

She knows that for two people to feel close, they have to really know each other well — not just the nice parts, but all of it. That means for you and your sweetheart to feel close, you need to know what's going on with her, and she needs to know what is going on with you. She needs to know what you're thinking, what you're feeling, what has been happening, what you've done, etc.

So if she has something important to her that's upsetting her, she wants you to know about it — not so you'll do something about it, but just so you *know*. She doesn't want to be alone with it. The two of you are sharing your lives together. She wants to feel connected, which means you need to know what is bothering her at the moment, so the two of you are in sync.

And when you try to make decisions or fix the problem as she is presenting it, you are cutting her off. You're shutting her up. She wants to talk about it because she wants you to know. So when you say, "Let's do this (a solution to the problem)," even though you are just being helpful and kind and caring and loving, she feels like you don't care, like you don't want to know what's going on with her, like you're trying to shut her up.

This is an important place where knowing the differences between the sexes can make a big difference. And for you to have a good relationship with her, you will have to temporarily set aside your bias for action once in awhile and *just* listen. Let her tell you what's going on with her. Don't interrupt. Don't offer advice. Do not give solutions. And do not take any action. Sounds like a torture, doesn't it? But it's not really. It is a gift you are giving her. And it will benefit you too, because you will understand her better.

This is not being phony. It is a choice you're making. It is something you are doing for her. It is something you're doing for love. It's something you do because you want to feel close to her and you want her to feel close to you. You're not *pretending* to care, you do actually care. But to show it, you have to rein in the action-oriented, highly-energetic thoroughbred you are riding (your testosterone-fueled body and brain).

This is not difficult. It takes some understanding, and it takes a little self-discipline, but it is physically easier than taking action to fix something. All you are doing is just *being there*. What could be easier than that? You're hardly doing anything.

Okay, what is the main point of this chapter? Simply this: That your woman wants to connect with you, and this means that you'll have to override your own natural tendency to avoid unpleasantness. You'll need to dive right into those difficult conversations — not because she wants you to be upset, but because she wants you to be *honest*. And the practice of the next chapter will greatly expand your level of honesty.

A Withhold a Day

For over three years now, every day I have told Klassy something she doesn't know about me. And it has changed my life. My honesty was an issue since we first met. Not that I am a liar. If you knew me personally, you would count me as one of your most trusted, honest friends. But there is another kind of dishonesty that comes from what we were just talking about in the last chapter — men want things to be pleasant, and that includes a desire to avoid saying something that may cause hurt feelings or disappointment or anger or just non-happiness.

Klassy has continually tried to persuade me to be more honest with her. And I have become progressively more open and honest with her throughout our marriage. But my withhold-a-day practice put me in a different league. The Honesty All-Stars.

When I first decided to tell her one withhold per day, I thought I would run out of things to say after a month or two. I mean, she already knew me really well. I was already very open with her. Surely after awhile there would be nothing left to say that she didn't know about me, right? But I never ran out, and still haven't to this day.

Every day I had to find something before I went to bed, and I often got to the very end of my day and realized I hadn't told her a withhold, so I would think of one and email it to her.

Gradually this became onerous, so I started paying more attention during the day, keeping a lookout for anything I could volunteer about myself that she didn't know.

The reward for getting this task off my day's to-do list compensated for the unpleasantness I anticipated for saying it (which was not always the case because other times what I had to say was not unpleasant). The desire to get my withhold *done* for the day was often greater than my desire to not cause a problem, so it was easier to say. The commitment to give a withhold a day, then, encouraged me to speak up.

After about three years, saying a withhold every day didn't seem like any problem at all. I was usually, without even trying, telling her several things in a day she didn't know about me.

What kinds of things am I talking about? For example, I've had a sore ear for several months. It feels like I have a mild ear infection, but the pain comes and goes so I haven't worried about it. But I realized the other day that it has been coming and going for a long time now and I began to worry about it. I realized I had never talked to her about it, so at my next opportunity, I told her about it.

Here's another example. She likes getting stuff at Costco. It saves a lot of money. But sometimes you have to buy a lot. One of those things is butter, so she stores the butter in the freezer. I have noticed it makes the butter have a slight freezer-burned flavor, so I made a point to tell her I don't like it and I'd rather pay a higher price for butter that tastes good.

These are minor things. But of course, sometimes I have major things to say, or things I more strongly do not want to tell her. That's one of the ways I discover a withhold: I ask myself what I *don't want* to tell her. Sometimes I just ask myself what she doesn't know about me — it could be good or bad. And then I just ponder the question for awhile. Usually I don't have to ponder very long.

She got a new perfume the other day. Right away there was something I didn't want to tell her. It was a perfume my first girlfriend wore. But I told her immediately. It was disappointing to her, like I figured it would be, because she liked the perfume.

Bringing You Closer

I recommend this practice to you. Try to come up with something you can tell her she doesn't know about you, and do it every day.

One of the side-effects is you'll feel more relaxed around her. You will have less and less to hide. And she will feel closer to you. She will know you better.

You will also feel a stronger sense of integrity because you know if you do something like flirt with a woman you work with, that it will be something she doesn't know about you, and you'll have to tell her about it, and since you don't want to have to tell her something like that, you'll just skip the flirting. It's not worth it.

You'll end up feeling better about yourself over time as you get more comfortable with being honest about yourself. And you will feel less guarded around her. You'll feel more open, relaxed, and free around her. And you'll feel closer to her. You'll *be* closer to her.

When you have something you don't want to tell her, it becomes a barrier to closeness. You have to pay attention to this thing you don't want her to know about you (to avoid accidentally revealing it). This makes you, to some degree, "not here," not present, not engaged in this moment, but "in your head" and "distant" instead. Your desire to be close to her will be diminished, and since feelings of love between you can only "flow" along the communication channel between you, when your communication is restricted, your affection for her is restricted too.

She is likely to notice your emotional distance and try to get you to reveal yourself, which will make you uncomfortable and make you pull back into yourself even more and you might even tell a lie to cover your withhold.

This is no way to live. You want to be close to her. She wants to be close to you. You want to be happy together, to speak freely to each other, to feel strong love and affection. The only way this can happen is if you are both open with each other, and that means sometimes you'll have to talk about stuff that will be unpleasant. That's the price you pay for a close, intimate, strong bond between you.

This all sounds good in theory, and I was convinced of it long before I started my withhold-a-day practice, but that daily practice really brought it home. It gave me something *specific* I could do. Having some vague thing I *should* do "more often" is not the same as having some specific thing — something small enough and specific enough that I can do it by the end of the day.

If you take on this commitment — and I hope you do, for your sake — you can go ahead and do easy ones at first. Think of things that are not upsetting in the least to share with her, as long as it's something about you that she doesn't know.

Some of the easier things to say are things you do for her that she may not know. And even this can benefit your relationship. Whenever Klassy and I used to share a sandwich, for example, I always cut the sandwich in half and gave her the better half — the top, rounded part. And I took the bottom, square part for myself. I love her and wanted to do this for her.

I never told her what I was doing. I just "assumed" she could tell. But then one day she asked me why I *always* took the good part of the sandwiches. She preferred the square half!

This was before my withhold-a-day practice. If I had been doing it then, I would have had the pleasure of telling her something I was doing for her that she didn't know about, and she would have revealed to me that she always felt I was being unfair, and half the time she should be able to have the good half, and we would have, from then on (as we have been doing since), each gotten the "best" half.

That's another benefit to the withhold-a-day practice. Stuff like this comes up and assumptions you've made that you didn't even realize you've made come to the surface and little things get cleared up. Big things too.

Part of your hesitancy about being honest is that while you may want to criticize something or say something you don't like, there are also plenty of things you do like, and maybe you think these kind of cancel each other out. You don't like it that she bitches at you sometimes, but on the other hand, she really looks out for you, so how can you complain?

But the truth is the truth, and what's really true is all of it. You don't want to say only the bad because that's not the only truth, so the answer is *to say the other truths too*. Say them all.

In other words, if you want to criticize her for something or complain about something, and you hesitate because you also really appreciate other things about her, say it all. Tell her you hesitate to say the criticism because it is also true that you appreciate all the positive things, then tell her the criticism and also the positive things. It will be a more complete truth, and it will certainly make it easier for her to hear the criticism.

What Do You Want?

One of the things that will come up again and again when you're saying a withhold a day is that you *want* something that she doesn't know about. This can be more difficult than it should be if you haven't taken the time to think about what you want.

You can't know what you really want unless you take the time to wonder about it. And you can't do this kind of thinking unless you're alone and it's quiet. So go for walks alone once in awhile. Go fishing alone. Spend uninterrupted time thinking about what you really want.

And then talk to her about what you want. She may very well bring up things you haven't thought of, or angles you haven't taken into consideration. Then think some more about it. Take the time and decide what you want.

Here is another fundamental difference between you two. She wants to *discuss* and you want to *decide*. You have a strong bias for *action*. But your bias for action, your chomping at the bit to get moving, to start *doing*, can also cause you to make more mistakes. You do more, but you also do more you regret later.

Your two natural propensities (yours and hers) are complimentary when you work together. So think about things, and discuss them with her, but then make decisions and take action. Indulge her desire to discuss things rather than pushing too hard to get to the decision and action part. Consider alternatives. Think about consequences. This will help you make *good* decisions and it will make her happier too.

And this issue of being willing to discuss things reminds me of an important point: You sometimes use withholds to maintain dominance and control. And dominance is anti-oxytocin. It is anti-connection.

Part of the reason you don't want to discuss things is that you want to take action, and discussing things just slows you down, miring you in details and contradictory facts and conflicting desires. If you keep the decision to yourself without discussing it, you can make a decision and move forward. So your withholding is one way to retain control and remain unencumbered by discussion. In other words, it functions as a way to dominate. You end up making decisions *for* her. This isn't being a good partner. It's more like being her dad or boss. Uncool.

Be Yourself

Discussing things doesn't come naturally to you. Saying withholds doesn't either. And you don't want to be a phony. You don't want to have to *make* yourself be something you're not. So where does "being yourself" come into play here? Because it is true, the only way to live is being yourself and not making yourself into something you're not.

Being yourself does not have to be in conflict with being the kind of man that makes her happy. The key bridge between the two is *honesty*. If you do not wish to do something but you do it *for her*, it is bad if you hide your true intentions and motivations, but it is good if you are honest about it.

Let's say it is my preference to keep to myself. In other words, keeping to myself would be "being my-self." If I was being "who I am" I would stay silent most of the time. If I prefer to keep to myself but in-stead I'm open and honest and expressive for her sake and for the sake of our relationship, it's good if she knows what I'm doing and why. But it's bad if I pre-tend I really *want* to be open and expressive, or that it's my natural way to be.

What does it mean to "be yourself" anyway? It means not pretending to be what you're not. It means being honest and not phony or manipulative. Telling a withhold a day will help you be yourself. It will help clear up those areas in your relationship where you are hiding what you *are* or pretending to be what you *aren't* or pretending to like what you don't like or pretending to want what you don't want.

Often when you say a withhold you will notice an immediate feeling of relief and closeness. You can re-lax. It's off your chest. She knows who you are. You no longer have to hide or pretend. It feels good.

If you want to have a great relationship with your woman, take on this discipline. Give her at least one withhold a day. It will take your relationship to a whole new level.

And to really complete this you will also inquire about her more. You will try to get *her* to tell *you* things you don't know about her. That's the subject of the next chapter.

Inquire and Disclose

Two of the things your woman does naturally that don't come naturally to you at all (but that really contribute to creating a close and happy bond) are inquiring and disclosing. You should take her lead on this and start doing more asking her about herself, and more disclosing things about yourself.

Men tend to share impersonal information. It may be information we feel passionate about, but it is about stuff out in the world, not about stuff going on inside us.

But information about what is going on inside you makes her feel closer to you, because she knows you better. You could talk to her all day about something you're passionate about, and it may be very interesting, but at the end of it, you don't have the pleasure of feeling known, and she doesn't have the satisfaction of knowing you any better.

Start noticing the difference between information and disclosures. "I talked to Randy and he said we could get that table from him tomorrow afternoon."

That's information.

"I talked to Randy today, and he said something that really pissed me off."

That's a disclosure.

"Someone wrote me an email today and said my article on sociopaths really made a difference to them."

That's information.

"It made me happy."

That's a disclosure.

"Last time we went to their place, we were there all afternoon."

That's information.

"I want to leave earlier this time."

That's a disclosure.

Why Does She Talk To You?

She often tells you about something that's bothering her because she wants you to know her. To you it seems like she's a damsel in distress and you want to rescue her. But she seems annoyed by your heroic attempts to help her, right? It can be very confusing. This is such a fundamental difference between men and women, I'm going to spend a few minutes to clarify this. She wants to be *known*. You want to fix it and make the unpleasantness go away. She wants to share what she feels. You want to give advice or get up and take care of it with *action*.

She wants to "feel felt." She wants to stop feeling alone with her problem. When you jump in with advice or decisions or actions, it seems like a very loving, caring thing from your point of view. But to her it seems like you don't want to connect with her, like you don't want to know her.

When researchers study what really helps people when they have problems, they find that giving advice and telling stories of your own similar difficulties — and all the other things men tend to do when they are trying to help their women — don't work. They don't help. What helps her the most is to be listened to. For you to just literally be there for her and be interested in her. She knows this. She is biologically and physically more aware of this fact than you ever dreamed of being.

When it comes to relationship stuff and connecting, she is the expert. You are a bumbling neophyte in this arena and it would be wise to follow her lead.

So when she talks to you and you find yourself *wanting* to help her, please remind yourself that what will really help her is one of the easiest things you can do — just relax and listen to her. This may be unnatural, but it's easy. You won't even break a sweat. Encourage her to talk to you in detail about the problem, including her feelings about it. Give her the time and space to talk about it, without giving her the impression you want to get this over with and do something more fun.

This is how to care about her.

You may not enjoy it at the time, but that doesn't matter. You're doing it for *her*. If you want to see her smile more often, it won't be by doing only what *you* find most fun or most pleasant. If you want both of you to be happier in the long run, this gift of your time and attention will really make a difference to her, will help her feel closer to you, will make her happier and feel more devoted to you, and she will help *you* in thousands of ways.

Rule of Thumb About Her

The following idea may not always be true, but it is a useful way to think: When she is down, it is because she doesn't feel felt (she doesn't feel listened to). When she eats too much and can't seem to stop herself, it is because she doesn't feel felt. When she is grumpy or depressed, she doesn't feel felt. When she stays up too late or doesn't take care of herself, she doesn't feel felt.

You want to do something to help her, don't you? When she seems distressed in any way, make the assumption that the source of the problem is that she doesn't feel felt, and what you can do for her is be there for her, get her to talk about what's bothering her, inquire, listen and make her feel not alone with her problems.

It won't seem to you that you are *doing* anything. But you will be doing the thing she needs most — helping her connect to you. You're helping her feel known and loved.

It doesn't matter what issue is bothering her. She will deal with it better if she feels she has a partner. She will cope better if she feels she's not alone with the problem, whatever it is. The feeling of not being alone is soothing and comforting. Talking about the problem helps her sort through her thoughts and feelings about it, and makes it easier for her to come up with possible solutions.

After talking about it for a while, if she starts asking you what you think, or if she shifts the conversation to brainstorming about ideas for possible solutions, *then* you can offer ideas. But always offer them tentatively and go out of your way not to "tell her what to do." Just offer ideas, if you can think of any.

But for the most part, avoid offering advice of any kind unless she directly asks you for it. And even then, add qualifications. Don't sound or look more certain about your advice than you really are. Just offer your ideas as "mere ideas" rather than "this is what you should do." Give her the respect of knowing she can decide for herself.

It Ain't Natural

You are biologically predisposed to under-inquire and under-disclose. But sometimes what comes naturally is not good for you. In the same way, you are biologically predisposed to seek out salt and sugar and to eat it when you can. For the millions of years of human evolution, salt and sugar were difficult to come by and very valuable. They were rare. Evolution built into our bodies a craving for them, so we would devour them whenever we came across them. But now that natural tendency is not good for us. So we do our best to try to eat more veggies than we really feel like eating because it's healthier.

In the same way, you will benefit by trying to inquire more and disclose more, against your natural tendency to do otherwise.

When you don't know what to do to help your relationship, think "inquire and disclose." Ask her something about her life or her feelings. Express curiosity about her, and when she answers, listen. Let her feel heard.

When you're in a difficult conversation with her, or whenever you don't know what to do or how to proceed in a conversation with her, think "inquire and disclose." Notice that inquiring comes first. That's a good rule of thumb. First inquire.

During upsetting conversations I used to either just keep my mouth shut or obsessively justify and explain myself. Neither of these is a good option, as I'm sure you've discovered for yourself. Neither of them help at all. Inquiring and disclosing, however, can help a great deal. It's a bit of a discipline, but just keep trying. Even being a *little* better at it is far better than not even trying.

Think in terms of *identity*: It makes change easier and more complete. Not "I try to inquire and disclose" but "I am an inquirer and a discloser." Or "I am the kind of man who inquires and discloses." Studies have found that framing a personal change in terms of identity can help you make changes more quickly and more permanently.

Change I Will to Will I?

Another thing that can help make changes last is to avoid having the feeling of forcing yourself. In a series of experiments, psychologist Ibrahim Senay demonstrated that there's a subtle difference between *wondering* whether you are going to do something and *deciding* you're going to do something, and that subtle difference can make a big difference. Studies show that *wondering* is more effective. In one experiment, subjects were about to work on some anagrams (rearranging the letters of a word to make another word — for example, changing "when" to "hewn" or "sauce" to "cause").

When two groups of subjects were told they were going to do anagrams, they were told in two different ways. One group was told to think about *whether or not* they would work on the anagrams. The other group was told *to think about the fact* that they would be working on anagrams.

Like I told you, that's a subtle difference. But after the experiment, those who *wondered* whether they'd do anagrams were able to successfully complete a lot more anagrams. They were more effective. The question "Will I?" worked better than "I will."

Senay went on to do other experiments, and they showed the same thing. In another study he measured the volunteers' ability to stick to an exercise program. Those who *wondered* whether or not they would exercise regularly actually exercised more regularly than those who were *determined* to do so! In writing about these experiments, author Wray Herbert wrote:

> These findings are counterintuitive. Think about it. Why would asserting one's intentions undermine rather than advance a stated goal? Perhaps, Senay hypothesized, it is because questions by their nature speak to possibility and freedom of choice. Meditating on them might enhance feelings of autonomy and intrinsic motivation, creating a mind-set that promotes success.

This principle has great implications for you when you're trying to inquire and disclose or when you're trying to speak her love language or turning toward all her bids for connection. If you wonder about it more than "try to make yourself do it" you will be more successful. Ask yourself, "I wonder if I can become a good inquirer and discloser?" rather than, "Today I will do more inquiring and disclosing!"

Being, Not Doing

Have you ever had moments, perhaps on a vacation, when you were relaxed, open, curious about her but not really going anywhere, but just wanting to be with her? This is the mindset that cultivates connection. It's not your usual state. Testosterone tends to override it with a restlessness and desire for action and progress.

But it is not impossible for you to create the conditions that would be conducive to a relaxed, open mindset.

Two things you can change to create conducive conditions are the circumstances and the state of your body.

The key factor for circumstances is that you create a long period of time when you have nothing to do. You're a busy man, no doubt. You've always got things to do, probably more than you could do even if you never slept. But think about this: When you go on vacation, you might have a week or two off from doing any of those things that "must be done" and the world does not fall apart. So it's not as cut and dried as it seems. Most of what you feel *must be done* doesn't actually *have* to be done, or at least not as urgently as you feel it does. One week-long vacation proves that point emphatically.

You can do the same thing with an evening together. Take the time off *psychologically*. Have no time pressure whatsoever for periods of time, and do this fairly often.

When you create a period of time with nothing you need to do, you can have conversations with her that drift aimlessly. And you can just be with her. That is creating circumstances conducive to connecting.

The other factor is the physical state of your body. If you feel agitated, it is not conducive to feeling relaxed, of course. So when you drink too much coffee, it will not be conducive. If you haven't had enough sleep, it won't be conducive either, because as soon as you feel relaxed, you'll get drowsy and how can you have a good conversation when you're falling asleep?

Exercise, particularly cardio workouts, can really help you relax and feel good in your body.

When you feel calm and relaxed, you are a better man. When you feel calm and relaxed, all of the following are *reduced*: greed, selfishness, anger, judgment and criticism, fear, deficiency motivations, feelings of revenge, agitation, anxiety, and frustration.

And when you feel calm, all these come more easily and naturally: forgiveness, compassion, peace, happiness, contentment, thoughtful decisions and actions, love, affection, appreciation, openness, balanced thinking, patience, and kindness.

To create the best, highest quality time with her, cultivate a state of mind and body that allows you to feel relaxed and at ease when you spend time with her.

What Can You Do?

Have you ever wondered what you could do that would make her happy? I'm sure you have. It's what almost every man wants: A happy woman. "What can I do to make her happy?" is the perennial question on a man's mind. But it's the wrong question. It puts your attention in the wrong field. The right question is, what can you *be* that will make her happier? Because you're a man, you focus on *doing*. Focus on being and you get different answers. What can you *be* that will bring her happiness?

Answer: Open.

You can be communicative — not about information, but about what you want and what you feel. Disclose. Be open. Open yourself up. Calm down and open up.

Being open may not come naturally for you, but you don't have to do it perfectly for it to make a difference. You don't even have to do it very well. Just do it more often than you do now, and she will be happier.

The Answer

The all-purpose, always helpful answer you have been looking for is "inquire and disclose." The answer to how to deal with an upset is inquire and disclose. The key to partnership is inquiring and disclosing. The way to intimate connection with her is inquiring and disclosing. The way to make her happy is inquiring and disclosing.

When you don't know what to do, inquire and disclose.

I once believed that if I'd already said a withhold once, then I didn't need to say it again. And this reveals another fundamental difference between men and women. I was thinking of a disclosure as giving information. She thinks of it as "what is true for me right now."

So let's say the kitchen table is a mess and it's her stuff there, and it annoys me. So I tell her. Three days later, the table is still a mess (or a mess again) and it *still* annoys me. I don't need to tell her, though, because I already told her, right? Wrong.

Sometimes when you say something, it is "off your chest" and now you feel complete with it. But sometimes you *don't* feel complete, or the issue keeps arising. You should disclose it again. Just be honest. What is true for you right now?

This has been one of the biggest confusions I had when I first began having relationships with women. She would sometimes tell me things that I knew were factually incorrect. She might say something like, "You don't care about me." She was telling me what she *felt* right then. She was disclosing. She wanted me to know her.

But I thought of it as *information*. And so I would try to correct her misunderstanding. I would point out something I did yesterday that proves I care about her. In other words, she told me what she was feeling at the moment, and I justified myself or tried to prove her wrong. We were talking two different languages. She felt unheard and unfelt. I felt unjustly accused and misunderstood.

When men accuse women of nagging, it comes from the same misunderstanding. Just because she already told you something important to her doesn't mean she doesn't feel it again today.

Save yourself these kinds of frustrations. Recognize that the answer is *inquiry and disclosure*. Recognize that telling her a withhold doesn't necessarily solve the problem. It only says what is true for you right now. It may be true for you again tomorrow, and needs to be said again. And recognize when she's upset and tells you something, she's not trying to tell you *facts*, but *feelings*. Just listen to her and recognize that this is what she is feeling at the moment. It doesn't mean she will feel it from now on. It doesn't mean she has forgotten all the great things she appreciates about you. Listen to what she's saying as a description of a feeling she's having right in this moment. Understand it. Acknowledge it. Don't try to do anything about it. Let her disclose herself.

Don't Stop, Add

It's more important to focus your attention on *adding* inquiry and disclosure than trying to *stop* doing what you naturally do. You will normally and naturally talk a lot, but you will be mostly sharing information. This doesn't really help with connection. So your first and most natural response will be to try to stop doing that. It's the wrong focus. Put your attention instead on *adding* more inquiry and disclosure in your communication.

Think of the conversation as a tennis game. If you just keep hitting balls, it eventually stops being fun for the other player. But you can say, "Hit one back to me" once in awhile. That is, you can inquire. You can express your curiosity about her, about what's going on with her, about what she's been doing and thinking and feeling, how her friends and family are doing, etc. Seek *emotional* information. It makes the tennis game more fun for her.

And she is interested in what's going on *within* you. What do you feel? When you're talking about something that happened, add how you *feel* about it.

Trying to stop doing something keeps your mind focused on the past, and focused on the negative, and focused on what you *don't* want. So re-focus your mind on what you want more of. Focus your mind on inquiry and disclosure. Leave the past behind and don't look back. Move forward into a new life with her.

Bottomless Well

When you give a withhold a day, you will discover something about yourself: You *always* have something *more* to disclose. And this is also true for her. That means *she* is also a bottomless well. There is always something more to find out by inquiring. You think you already know her. So it doesn't occur to you to inquire. But the only reason you think you know her is because testosterone makes you feel more confident than is justified, more certain about what you think, and tends to make you overlook what you've deemed "not relevant." You don't naturally notice everything. You've got a built in kind of tunnel vision.

For all these reasons, you won't normally inquire very much except in the beginning of a relationship because you don't yet know her. One of the reasons relationships are so good in the beginning is because you don't yet feel you know her, so you are interested in her and want to know all about her. But then once you think you've got her figured out, you stop inquiring.

But guess what? She has endless depth and is always changing. She has a lot about her you still don't know, and no matter how open she is with you, this is always true. So inquire.

Inquiry can be done in the spirit of interest and curiosity, the way you did it when you were first getting to know each other. Or inquiry can be done in the spirit of an Inquisition. Of course, you don't want it to feel like a cross-examination to her, which is what it will feel like if you are "forcing yourself" to inquire, or if you're doing it under a time pressure or out of obligation. Your state of mind and body are critical here.

Inquiry, to be the wonderful thing it can be, needs to come out of a feeling of love, affection, and curiosity. You can do two things to make this happen. You can get your body and the circumstances conducive to relaxed conversation, and you can think about her and wonder about what you don't know about her, so when you're with her, you'll have lots of things you want to know about her.

Acknowledgment

An acknowledgment can, and perhaps *should* always be, a disclosure. In other words, you would not just say *what* you appreciate, but *why* you appreciate it. What did it make you feel? What difference does it make in your life? Did it make you proud of her? Happy to be married to someone like that? Disclose.

As a man, inquiring and disclosing is something you chronically underdo. And just like most human beings, acknowledgment is something you chronically underdo as well.

If you were in the habit of inquiring and disclosing, you would be calm and assertive. Disclosing — simple honesty — is naturally assertive and calm. Honesty makes you feel calm because you're not hiding anything. You're standing on solid reality. You don't have to try to remember what you're not saying, so you are at ease with yourself.

It Doesn't Come Naturally Any More

Sometimes you'll feel like you have to try to remember what "should" come naturally. For example, inquiring and disclosing should be written plain in your DNA. In fact, it probably is because you were female in the beginning. But testosterone has pushed you out of your innate wisdom. Nature has her reasons, but it doesn't necessarily make your life any happier.

Testosterone interferes with your natural knowing that connecting as the most important thing that happens in life. It's still important to you. It's the most important thing there is, but you often don't *act* like it because you are high on testosterone and it distorts your orientation and view of the world. So you might feel alone or alienated sometimes, without knowing why.

Do you want to return home? This is one of the paths that will take you home, where you will feel relaxed and connected: Become a man who inquires and discloses.

Impatience is the Key

What do men do rather than connect? We get stuff done. We *do* things. We stay busy and active, or we've got something to watch on TV that involves someone *else* doing active things. We are addicted to action.

I am not knocking it. I love action. It makes me happy. But remember that the truth is, even for men, love is the most important thing there is. It is the most meaningful thing, the thing that most deeply matters to you, and the most significant source of your happiness. Without love, life has no juice, no aliveness, no joy.

Okay then. Action must take second place. Don't worry, you'll still have plenty of opportunities to indulge your lust for action. But you have to make sure *love comes first*. Connection comes first. They trump whatever action you want to take.

So when your woman makes a bid for connection, do your best to drop whatever you were about to *do* and *be* there for her. You will feel impatient when this happens. You will have a negative feeling of wanting to "get this over with" so you can get on with what you were planning on doing.

That's impatience.

And it gets in the way of connecting. It is one of the primary ways testosterone impedes connection. Testosterone gives you an energetic, action-orientation that pushes you to rush through those opportunities to connect, which means *you're not really connecting*. You can't connect in a hurry.

What can you do about this? You can *let go*. That's how to become less impatient.

I don't like to use the word "patient." It conjures up discomfort for me. It brings to mind a deep, frustrated sigh as I try to "wait patiently" for something. That is *not* what we're aiming for here.

For you to really *be* here and connect with her, you can't be even internally tapping your foot. And for that to happen, you have to *truly* let go of what you were about to do. And reaffirm to yourself that this is more important. Love is more important. *She* is more important.

You don't have to withhold what you feel. In fact, you should not. You don't have to say it at the time, although sometimes it might be appropriate (if you don't have to interrupt her to say it). But you can certainly say, "I was about to go check my email, but you are more important. What do you want to talk to me about?" And let it go, sit down and give her your full, relaxed attention.

Once she knows what you're doing, you can just be with her and connect. Give her your attention. When a thought comes up about what you were going to do, let it go. Let the task go for now. This will *relax* you. If it *doesn't* relax you   if it's really something urgent that needs to be done now — share *that* with her, but while letting her know *why* you need to interrupt her and that you will give her your undivided attention when you're done.

And then make sure you do.

But if you have something that really isn't urgent, but still you can't seem to let it go when she wants to connect with you, then do a little soul searching as soon as you get the chance. Go on a long walk, or sit by yourself in a quiet place and ask yourself some questions. Do you really care about this woman? Do you want her to be happy? Do you want to have a close, loving relationship?

If the answers are sincerely yes, yes, and yes, then letting go of impatience is something you'll find easier to do next time.

But what if what she wants to talk about is not interesting to you?

Answer: Because *she* cares about it, that's good enough. She cares about it and she wants you to know her. She wants to connect with you. And she wants to *feel known* by you.

Think about that, and then let your impatience go.

Although this whole book has been oriented to what you can *do* differently, in a way it's not what you *do* that really matters. It's what you *value*. Changing what you do without changing what you value won't work. And once you change what you value, you don't have to focus so much on your behavior. It will flow naturally out of your values.

And you don't really need to *change* your values. You need only to be clear about what you really value. Testosterone interferes with this. It is like a drug that impairs your ability to remember what you really care about.

That's why you need some time by yourself. Time spent by yourself thinking about what you really care about will allow you to clarify your values. This is not something you do once and then you're all set. Every once in awhile, throughout your life, you should take some time and clarify what you want most. It reboots you.

The old Windows software used to have a flaw. Every time you opened and closed a program, Windows captured a little of the RAM memory. After awhile, your computer would start to slow down as you ran out of working memory. But then when you rebooted, all your memory was back. It refreshed your computer, making it work the way it was supposed to work. Microsoft has fixed that glitch, but *you* still have the same glitch.

If you don't clarify your values, if you don't take the time to think about what you really want, after awhile, you lose your enthusiasm. You're just going through the motions. You're doing what you decided a long time ago you wanted to do. Now it just feels like something you *have* to do.

When this happens, you just need to reboot yourself by taking a little time and starting fresh. Starting right now, what do you really want? What do you really care about?

You'll usually find that what you really care about stays consistent over your lifetime. But it's one thing to *remember* that you cared about it. It's an entirely different experience to be freshly aware that you care about it now. It brings your values to life. It gives you an enthusiasm and an earnest appreciation for it in the present.

So when you're letting your impatience go, but you just don't have any enthusiasm for it anymore, take some time by yourself and think about what you really want. Think about what you really care about. Are the things you want to do *really* more important than your relationship?

Clear your head, get your priorities straight, and you'll be able to let those things go when it's the right thing to do. And you won't do it grudgingly, but with commitment.

You can summarize this whole book with the principle: *Care about her as your number one priority.*

Where the Rubber Meets the Road

Here's how to become less impatient: Notice what you want to rush off to, realize love is more important than anything, and let go of what you wanted to rush to.

Your urge to move is testosterone impeding what is most important to you. To behave consistent with your values — which is a fundamental principle of mental and emotional health — you would let that stuff go. Letting it go demonstrates that nothing is more important than your connection with her.

Another way to deal with impatience is to think of the feeling of impatience as a sign you haven't said something. Especially something you want.

Since you have such a strong action bias, you may have to deliberately take the time to think about what you want.

Three things will consistently arise that you will feel impatient about: Something *you* planned on doing, something she told you *she* planned on doing, and your desire to make a decision and get moving rather than linger in the "undecided and still considering possibilities" stage. This is testosterone's bias for action impeding your ability to have a close relationship.

Notice your feeling of impatience, then either let it go or say something about it. For example, "I just realized I had better start getting ready for work."

Thinking

Let's talk about decisions. Men and women have very different natural proclivities when it comes to decision making. When *you* are trying to decide, you tend to settle for the first good answer. This is your bias for action interfering with your ability to make good decisions. So you tend to get more done but you also tend to make more mistakes. You want to finish thinking and get into motion.

When *she* tries to make a decision, when she comes up with a good answer, *she keeps thinking* because she knows if she keeps thinking, she might come up with an even *better* answer. This is one of the things that frustrates you in conversations with her. She wants to discuss. You want to make a decision and start getting something done.

Advertisers have found that if they want to appeal to a man, they only have to give him one good reason. But to appeal to a woman, they have to give *several* good reasons.

When you're discussing a possible decision with her, you will tend to feel impatient. You want to just make a decision. But if the decision has consequences, her propensity to keep thinking (to see if she can come up with an even better idea) is smart. It is what you would do if testosterone were not driving you to get up and get moving. So when you're discussing something with her, or when you're thinking on your own, try to take any good idea you come up with as "the best one *so far*" and see if you can come up with something even better.

The more important the decision, the more time it's worth to think about it and discuss it. This change in your attitude will make you less impatient.

Here's how it works: You will try to think up a solution. You'll consider a few possibilities and when you come up with one that's pretty good, you'll want to get to work on it. But instead, write it down and set it aside. And see if you can come up with something even better. Give yourself a target: "I will come up with ten possibilities before I decide." Or "I will keep coming up with ideas until 6:30 before I stop and decide which one I like best."

This is classic brainstorming. This is how you get really good ideas. And it works even better if both of you are doing this together. Your different perspectives will help broaden the horizon of possibilities and your new ideas and new angles can help you both come up with possibilities you wouldn't have thought up if you were brainstorming alone.

You'll often find your best ideas are the ones you come up with after you think you've already come up with every possibility. It's almost as if your brain gives you the most obvious answers first. But if you keep asking the question, *then* it starts digging in and being creative.

The Key to the Key

See if this sounds familiar to you: The thing that makes me most impatient is my standards. I have standards for myself about how much I should be accomplishing, or how quickly. And if I'm not meeting those standards, then I feel I'm "behind." So I become impatient. Is this something you do as well?

If so, you can use the same method I mentioned earlier: Notice what you are rushing off to (when you feel impatient) and let it go.

I wanted to mention how standards might be making you impatient because it made such a big difference to me. Once I realized what it was, I became more pervasively relaxed. Once I realized that the standards that gave me such a feeling of pressure, and of being behind, were just ideas *I made up*, I realized I had a choice. And it seemed ridiculous that I created standards that made me unhappy. They made me feel *rushed*. They caused me to want to cut off conversations with the person I care about most. It was just foolish, and if you're making the same mistake, I suggest you really think about your standards. You don't need those standards to "make" yourself get things done. You naturally *want* to get things done. You can let those standards go. Or at least put them in their place (second place — love is first).

Don't Be Brief

Another way impatience shows up is that men tend to be efficient with their communication — *too* efficient. You don't give her enough information. It's a strange thing, because sometimes when you are talking about something you're enthused about, you can talk a lot. But on other subjects, you have a tendency to say as little as possible, and assume she'll know what's going on or she'll understand your intentions, rather than taking the time to spell them out for her. This is a function of the way your brain developed in the womb, combined with testosterone's ongoing effect on you.

What you can do about it is make an effort to give her more information than you think is really necessary.

For example, I was going to put some batteries away and I thought I knew where she kept them, but I wasn't sure, so I left them out for her to put away. Normally, I would not let her know why I did this. I would just assume she would know. But whenever possible, don't make your woman guess. Say it.

Klassy wasn't around and I had to leave, so I wrote a note next to the batteries that said, "I left the batteries out because I wasn't sure where they went and didn't want to put them in the wrong place."

And even this was kind of brief. More than I *would* have said in the past, but still I could have added more, and that's the way you should think about this — give *lots* of information. Don't be brief. I could have told her I thought I remembered she kept the batteries in a different place now but wasn't sure.

She probably wondered how I could have forgotten where we keep the batteries, but she has a better memory for the locations of things. And I have something else working against me — a better focus.

Men have a better ability to concentrate our attention singlemindedly. This is great for many purposes, but it also means sometimes you don't really record information that you don't think is relevant at the time. Of course, sometimes you don't realize it *will* be relevant to you at some future time, because you can't always predict that.

But sometimes she tells you things that somehow your mind does not register as "memorable" and later she will say, "I told you that already." She doesn't understand how you could have forgotten it. Her mind works differently.

She tends to remember everything. *You* tend to remember what you think is relevant. She tends to listen to everything. You tend to listen to what you think is relevant. She tends to notice everything. You tend to notice what you think is relevant.

And she tends to tell you everything. You tend to tell her what you think is relevant.

You can try to overcome this tendency of yours, and you should, but you will never be as good at it as she is naturally, no matter how hard you try. But you should try anyway. It makes a difference to her. It prevents misunderstandings. It keeps her from explaining your actions to herself in an inaccurate way. It helps her know you and understand you better. It helps her come up with good ideas. It helps her make better decisions. It helps her support you better.

Listening

Does your woman sometimes feel unheard? That's a lonely, depressing, frustrating, demotivating feeling for anyone, especially a woman. And you have the power to relieve her of that feeling. The only thing that stands in your way is impatience.

But if you are turning toward her bids for connection and if you're letting your impatience go, you will be giving her what she wants — a feeling of being heard, being felt, being understood, and a feeling that you're on her side, you're there for her.

Listen to her disclosures. Inquire. *Ask* her for disclosures. Find out what she feels, what she thinks today. And listen — not for information, but so you really *know* her. A great deal of pleasure and happiness await you both on the other side of your impatience.

The Counterpoint to the Coolidge Effect

President Coolidge was with his wife on a tour of a chicken farm, going in two separate tour groups. In one part of the tour, Mrs. Coolidge asked how many times a single rooster copulated per day. The answer was several times a day. She quipped, "Tell that to Mr. Coolidge."

Later, someone told President Coolidge. He responded, "Was it the same chicken every time?" When told the answer was no, Coolidge said, "Tell that to Mrs. Coolidge."

Breeders of cows find the same thing: A bull can copulate with a single cow, and when he is done, he will not copulate anymore that day. But if you put a new cow in the pen with him, he will copulate again. Take her out and put another in, and he will copulate *again*.

In scientific circles, this has become known as the "Coolidge Effect," and it applies to most mammals.

Male mammals have extra ardor for a female they haven't yet mated with.

Of course, this is kind of depressing for a couple who wants to remain happily monogamous.

But a flood of new research on oxytocin has found some good news. In experiments with mice, researchers have found that when copulation *lasts* for awhile, males prefer to mate again with the female they have already mated with — they prefer her to novel females.

The key was extending arousal. A male and a female were put into a cage that was separated down the middle with holes between the two halves of the cage. The holes were big enough for the female mouse to go through, but too small for the male to fit through.

In that situation, she gets to set the pace of sex, and she takes it slower than he does. She goes to "his" side and they mate some, and then she escapes into the other side before he has a chance to finish. Then she comes back and they do it some more. Finally, he climaxes and the sex is over.

Later, when he is put into a cage with her and other females he hasn't mated with, the male prefers to mate with the female he's *already* mated with — directly the opposite of the Coolidge Effect. Why? Researchers are fairly sure it's because of the elevated level of oxytocin in his blood that occurs during the extended mating.

A state of arousal makes the body release oxytocin into the blood stream. Extended arousal produces *extra* oxytocin, and *oxytocin is a bonding hormone*. It is involved in feelings of attachment, devotion and affection.

Your own experience can demonstrate that the same principle applies to humans. If you extend your arousal, if you go at a slower pace than you want, or if she teases you and *makes* you go slower or makes your sexual interludes last longer, the two of you will become more attached to each other and more affectionate toward each other. Your feelings of devotion to each other will rise.

What you are doing is raising the oxytocin level for both of you for a longer period of time, which means if a "normal" sexual interlude lasts twenty minutes, you each get, say, two cubic centimeters of oxytocin released into your blood during that time. But if you make the arousal last *forty* minutes, you get four cubic centimeters.

What Does it Mean to Be a Partner?

You are a selfish bastard. I know you don't like hearing that when she is yelling it at you, especially when you have recently demonstrated your selfishness, but we are just speaking here man to man, and we can admit it to each other, can't we?

It's not that you are *totally* selfish. You care about her and you probably do a lot for her, and you do it just for her sake. But *compared to her*, you *are* selfish.

When you tell her your goals, she takes them on as something she cares about and she tries to help you attain them. But sometimes when she tells you *her* goals, you don't really hear them. And sometimes even when you *do* hear them, you take them on as something that you hope she will accomplish and if she does, you'll be happy for her. If she asked you to do something specific for her tomorrow that would help her accomplish her goal, you would gladly and enthusiastically do it.

But that's not *nearly* as cooperative and "partnery" as what she does, is it?

Men are missing the "cooperation hormone." There isn't really any such thing, but if there was, you'd find men have less of it than women. Not that we *can't* cooperate — we just aren't as good at it as women are naturally. Really, it's more like we would be more naturally cooperative and "partnery," but testosterone interferes with our tendencies toward partnership.

But you can be a better partner than you are right now, and if you were, your life would be better and she would be more satisfied with you as a mate. She would feel more cared about, and she would feel more connected to you.

So start today being alert to opportunities — when she openly expresses something she wants, a goal she has, something she is planning, and make a commitment to yourself that you will support that goal. Not that you will take over and *make* her do it, or become an overseer, but commit yourself to staying aware of her goals and plans, and support her in every way you can that doesn't take away her ownership of the goal.

Stay *aware* of her goals. Remember her goals. Keep them in mind. Be *committed* to them. And if you have trouble keeping them in mind, use memory aids like reminders or calendars or personal organizers or PDAs or whatever you can use that will help. Make it your responsibility as a partner to remain aware of her goals.

This is the most basic principle of partnership.

When you are unaware of her goals, you are not merely unhelpful, you actually *impede* her. Your obliviousness prevents her from achieving her goals. *You* become an obstacle.

The reason you impede her is because of *her* supportiveness. She is aware of your goals naturally, and is supportive of them. She is attuned to you. She has her attention on you, and when you ignore or forget *her* goals, it not only communicates a message that you are not interested in her, you can actually derail and deflect her from fulfilling *her* goals by simply doing what you do naturally — trying to accomplish your own goals.

So stay aware of her goals. That's being a partner.

Rudder and Sail

Klassy uses an analogy for how women and men can be partners for each other. Women are like the rudder — guiding the direction. Men are like the sail — giving power and speed to that direction. Neither is better than the other. And both are necessary to get where you want to go.

Which of you is more important? Which of you is superior? These are meaningless questions in the same way they are meaningless when talking about a rudder and sail. You need *both* to make it work, and they only fulfill their function when they work together.

Work together with her making good things happen. That's where the happiness is. You be the sail. Let her be the rudder.

Should you be devoted to her happiness? No. That is out of balance and won't work. *Your* happiness must be taken into consideration just as much. But being devoted to only your own happiness is out of balance too. But if you're dedicated to being her partner, that works beautifully. When you are a good partner — when you work in concert with her, when you coordinate what you do with what she does — she will be happy more often. And so will you.

When you are joined with her, looking out for her, caring about her, affiliating and cooperating with her, aware of your highest and deepest value — love — she will be happy more often. So if you want to be devoted to her happiness, be devoted to being a great *partner*. Be aware of her goals and act in concert with her — not with her being the boss, and not with you being the boss. Partners.

See the Best in Her

Another aspect of being a good partner is to see and acknowledge the best in her. A good general rule of thumb is to "acknowledge what you want more of." The natural way to do things is to ignore what you like and complain about or criticize what you don't like. But that doesn't work very well, as you have probably discovered already.

A better way is to go out of your way to notice what she does that you like and make sure you tell her you appreciate it.

You can be on the lookout for whatever you want. So be on the lookout for the very best in your woman

— the noble qualities, the kindness, the sweetness, whatever you like. And really appreciate those qualities when she displays them. Reward her for them.

Bring out her best. See the best in her. See her good intentions. This is what a good partner does.

Deliberate Cultivation of Love

Feelings of affection can be *cultivated* by loving actions on your part — acts of loyalty, acts of devotion, acts of love.

Before Ulysses S. Grant became the most celebrated general of the Civil War (and then President of the United States for two terms), he often struggled financially.

At one point in his life, he was trying his hand at farming. He had three slaves his father in law had loaned to him. One of the slaves was Mary Robinson. She cooked for Grant and his wife, Julia, and kept in touch with them for the rest of her life.

"I have seen many farmers," said Robinson, "but I never saw one that worked harder than Mr. Grant." But he was failing anyway, finding it impossible to make a living.

Robinson recalled an incident during this time that illustrates perfectly an act of loyalty by Grant's wife, Julia. "At one time he was very poor," said Robinson. "but both his wife and himself always looked on the bright side of things. One day — I will never forget the circumstances — Mrs. Grant was sitting in a large rocking chair talking to some of her relatives about family matters. She referred to the financial embarrassment of her husband and then added: But we will not always be in this condition. Wait until Dudy (meaning Mr. Grant) becomes President. I dreamed last night he had been elected president. The rest all laughed and looked upon it as a capital joke. The idea that her husband, who was then a very poor farmer, would ever become president of the United States. Mrs. Grant always had great confidence in her husband, and she never relinquished the belief that he was destined to become one of the greatest men in the nation."

Not only would an act of loyalty like that inspire Grant and make *him* feel more devoted to his wife, but acts of loyalty, acts of love, acts of devotion like that cause *the person doing it* — in this case, Mrs. Grant — to *feel* more loyalty, love and devotion too. The action itself strengthens those feelings.

If you treated your woman like you were newly in love, it would tend to *cause* feelings similar to when you were newly in love.

In many ways, relationships are self-feeding loops. Something you do makes her feel a certain way, which causes her to do something that makes you feel a certain way, which causes you to do something that strengthens her feelings, which causes her to do something that strengthens *your* feelings, round and round, whether they are positive feelings or negative.

You will feel a great *pleasure* in expressing loyalty. Whenever you get a chance, take actions and say words that demonstrate your loyalty and devotion to her. It will make you both happier.

Think About Her

You have a tendency to focus on your goals. And that's great. Don't stop doing that. But add something: Just *think* about her more. Wonder about her. What does she need? What is she doing tomorrow? What can you do that would help her? How does she feel? What is on her mind?

And ponder her disclosures. Think about what she has told you and try to fully grasp her experience. That would really help her, and would bring you closer.

When She's in a Bad Mood

Here's the scenario: You have done something wrong, and it has set off a spiral down for your woman. She is now thinking of everything you've *ever* done wrong, and all the things that are wrong with her life in general, and all the things that are wrong with your relationship.

She says some unpleasant things, and your thin veneer of patience and forgiveness has been peeled off in the blast, and then *you've* replied with some unpleasant things of your own.

One of you stomps away and there you sit — upset, bewildered, feeling both sorry and angry, and wondering how it came to this?

What should you do?

The first thing you need to decide on is your goal. I suggest you make your goal helping her deal with what's bothering her.

You might be thinking, "But I need help too. What about me?" Here's a little-known difference between the sexes: Men are over it faster. It usually takes a woman longer to "recover" from an argument. Men move on faster. We are more willing to more quickly let it go and forget about it. So once the two of you are upset, the person in the best position to help return you both to sanity is *you*. With great power comes great responsibility.

Give up on any self-serving goals you might have. Set your own desires aside for the moment and do something altruistic: Help her deal with what was upsetting her in the first place.

The first thing you know right off the bat is that one of the things bothering her is that you did something wrong, so deal with that first. Ask her why she feels the way she does. Listen for as long as she wants to talk. And if you can, promise not to do it again, or at least acknowledge that it was a mistake and you'll *try* not to do it again.

And if you feel bad about it, tell her.

And then do something to make up for it. Do something for her that she would like. If you can't think of anything, then give it some thought. Brainstorm. Come up with lots of ideas and see if you can think of something that would let her know you care about her.

One of the best things you can do for her is to really listen well. And when you listen to her, make it clear you want to help her. Stating your intention aloud helps you stay focused on it, and reassures her about your intentions.

Now you might be thinking, "Of *course* I want to help her," but if you watched a video of what you say and how you say it when she is upset with you, I'll bet you would agree it doesn't *look* like you want to help her. It looks more like someone trying to defend himself.

So put your head in the right place and *declare* your commitment to help her. Say it, and then keep your focus on it. Don't let anything she says or does deflect you from your commitment.

While she is speaking, accept her emotions. Accept her expressions. *Do not correct her if she exaggerates.* This is how she wants to communicate at the moment, and this is how she feels at the moment. Try not to get defensive about it or depressed about it. The gift you can give her right now is to accept her *as she is* in this moment. Remind yourself, if you must, that this is probably not her opinion or feelings all the time. It's just how she feels right now. Do not try to stop her expressions or make fun of them or repress them.

Ask her about her situation. Ask her *all* about her situation. The best thing you can do to help someone who is upset is to be extremely interested in the situation upsetting her and the feelings and thoughts she has about her circumstances. Do not let her be brief. Do not let her make a long story short. Get all the details.

What you're doing is allowing her to think about her situation and process it, and in so doing, you are helping her come to grips with it.

You don't need to give advice. In fact, you probably shouldn't. She's capable of dealing with her own problems if she can have a little time to think about them, and that's just what you're helping her have.

I suggest that whenever one of you stomps away in anger that you immediately sit down and read this chapter.

Let's reacap. What can you do when your woman is in a bad mood? Do something for her that she would really like. And listen to her. Tell her you want to help. Fully accept whatever way she expresses herself. And be interested in her situation and her feelings about it.

Moods Are Contagious

Your mood affects her. So being in a good mood is something you can do that really makes a difference to her, to both of you, and to your relationship in the long run. Your good moods will make her bad moods less likely, and your health and feeling of well-being will make it easier for you to handle her bad moods diplomatically. Given all this, when you don't know what to do, when you seem at the end of your rope, do something that will make you *healthier.*

And the rest of the time, try to take care of your health and body. Eat well, exercise, get enough sleep. It has a big impact on your general feeling of well-being and happiness, and therefore has an impact on hers. Particularly cardio exercise. It has the most positive effect on your mood, and it doesn't take much cardio to improve your general feeling of well-being for the entire day.

When you don't feel good, you're not as loving or as giving. That's true for everyone. And whether or not you feel good has a lot to do with how well you take care of your health. You can exercise and be responsible for your food and sleep as a loving act, as something you do for *her*.

And when you're feeling good, connect with her. We will talk about what that means to her in the next chapter.

What She Wants When She Wants to "Connect"

I am a fan of a little column in *Men's Health* called "Ask The Girl Next Door." She gives very sensible answers to questions men ask. In one of her answers, she said something we men should memorize, or carve onto a stone memorial and place in the center of our homes.

The man's problem was basically, "When I leave on a week trip and get back, my girlfriend is distant." Nicole Beland (the girl next door) told the man he should call his girlfriend every day while he is on his trips. And then Nicole says the thing we should memorize:

> "Long, laid-back conversations that wander from one random topic to another feel the most intimate and gratifying."

Why would a woman find this kind of conversation the most intimate and gratifying? Because the mind-set of a man who is having that kind of conversation is exactly what she's looking for: A man who just wants to be with her. Any other kind of conversation is purpose-focused. It's trying to "get somewhere." It's trying to gain information or give information or persuade or make something happen or get it over with.

A long, laid-back conversation that wanders from one random topic to another can only be done by someone who is happy to be where he is, and just happy to be with her.

That's the attitude she wants in a conversation, and that's the attitude she wants during sex. It's the opposite of efficiency, goal-orientation, and time-pressure. Those have no place in good sex or in good conversations.

Of course, if you have this kind of conversation in order to please her, that's goal-orientation. The only way to really do this authentically, in a way that will actually satisfy both of you (which is the real goal here), is for you to genuinely realize that you can both experience a sense of timeless pleasure by stepping out of the efficiency-oriented, goal-oriented, time-oriented mode for awhile.

And the way to realize that authentically is to start paying attention. Notice the unique pleasure of just being right where you are when you're in the midst of a sexual interlude or conversation. Tune into the pleasure of it. Once you notice it and recognize it for the sublime experience it really is, you'll find it irresistible, and you'll want more of it.

Connection is the most important thing. Do not drift from this great truth. You knew it when you first met, and you spent all the time you could with your woman. The rush of hormones at the beginning temporarily overwhelmed your testosterone, and created an opening, a magical period of time when you were living from the truth that love is the only thing that really matters.

But now the natural window has closed. And you act like all the other stuff is more important. But the truth is still the truth.

What you need is more being and connecting. And less doing and thinking. This is not all-or-nothing. You should not give up doing and thinking. But the influence of testosterone tends to push you out of balance. So add a little more *being* and *connecting* to bring yourself into balance.

Relaxation Versus Goals

This is a distinction you've probably never made, but it is fundamental to the way *she* perceives the world: A goal-orientation is the opposite of relaxation. When you are just here now and enjoying the moment with her, you have temporarily set aside your goal-fixation, and that will affect her. It will bring her happiness, and it will bring you happiness too.

Men dominate in every way imaginable. This fundamental truth is not easy for you to see because it has always been that way for you. It is a male-dominated, goal-oriented world. She has lived her whole life in a largely alien world with alien values and she has also gotten used to it. But in her heart she has never let go of the truth — that love and connection are more important than anything else. So when *you* relax and be with her and connect, when you set aside your goal-orientation for awhile, it is a very special experience for her. Relaxation is outside this world, in a sense. It's where connection happens.

You can help her reach that special state beyond time. The more often you do, the more you will see her smile.

Make it Real

It's one thing to know and understand the information in this book. It's another thing altogether to use the ideas to change your relationship for the better. What does it take to make real change in your life? The main key is *remembering* the new ideas at the right time. And since there are a lot of ideas in this book, this could be difficult.

To make it easier, I've got one more idea for you. It's a method to help the information cross the boundary between the time you read the principle and the time that principle could be applied in your life. It's a way to help you remember the principles when you could really use them. It's a meta-principle.

Here's the method: Ask yourself, "What principle might help here?" When you want to connect, or when things are going badly in your communication with your woman, or when you feel exasperated or don't know what to do, ask yourself, "What principle might help here?" What we've got in this book is a collection of principles. Here they are in a nutshell:

1. The all-purpose answer is to inquire and disclose.

2. Every day, tell her something she doesn't know about you.

3. Turn toward all her bids for connection.

4. Discover her love language and use it when communicating your love to her.

5. Do something that will raise her oxytocin level.

6. Listen to her as the expert when she says anything about relationships.

7. Interrupt her less during conversations.

8. Remind yourself that love is the most important value in life. Testosterone makes it hard for you to keep this in mind.

9. Respond enthusiastically to anything she is happy about.

10. Don't worry about doing any of this perfectly.

11. Experiment with taking all her suggestions for a set period of time.

12. Experiment with running every decision by her.

13. Experiment with imagining the world from her eyes.

14. Experiment with speaking with excessive accuracy.

15. Watch *Dog Whisperer* and *Don Juan*.

16. Experiment with assuming you don't already know all about her.

17. Experiment with noticing something you have never noticed before about her.

18. Be more willing to converse with her when it is unpleasant — stop trying so hard to make it pleasant. Just try to be honest about what you are feeling and what you want.

19. Don't let your arguments escalate. Pull yourself away and take a break.

20. When she is unhappy, assume she needs to be heard and felt. Ask her to tell you all about it. Don't interrupt. Don't give advice. Don't try to fix it. Just listen with all your heart.

21. Be open with her.

22. When your impatience rears its ugly head during conversations, notice what you want to rush off to, and *let it go*.

23. When communicating with her, don't be brief — give detail.

24. Stay aware of her goals and support her goals. Think about her goals.

25. See the best in her.

26. Demonstrate your love for her with acts of loyalty and devotion — this cultivates feelings of affection in you.

27. Take care of yourself physically so you feel good, because moods are contagious.

28. Create conditions conducive to long, laid-back conversations that wander from one random topic to another.

The more you become familiar with the principles, the more useful the meta-principle will become because some principles will be more useful or applicable than others for any given situation. You do not want to be like the guy who only has one tool and tries to use it for everything. As the saying goes, when all you have is a hammer, everything looks like a nail.

You may *eventually* be able to ask the question and intuitively know to turn toward her bid or pull yourself away from the argument or disclose something about yourself, and it will be the perfect thing to do right then.

But at first, when you ask yourself the question, "What principle might help here?" you will, of course, not have this book memorized, so *refer to the book* for the answer. Keep the book handy and literally look it up. Use this book as a field manual or reference book. Ask yourself the question and then browse through the book to find the answer or just look over the list in this chapter. What would be a good principle to apply right at this time and in this situation?

Continually asking the question and looking up an answer will train you over time. After looking up an answer twenty, thirty, a hundred times, you'll begin to be so familiar with the principles that a good answer will start popping into your head when you ask the question. But in the meantime, use this book. Keep it around. Don't worry about memorizing anything.

So really, all you have to remember is to ask yourself the question, "What principle might help here?" And browse the book for answers. Eventually you will know what to do without the book.

Another good question I've used in the same way is, "What one thing could I do right now that would make things better?" You can see that the question is purely positive. There are usually lots of things that might improve the situation. Pick one and do it. This doesn't aim to make things perfect. It does not try to solve all the problems. It's only a small step, but a step in the right direction, and often that's all you need to turn things around.

Pick the question you like best, and use it often. When in doubt, or when you're stressing, or when she seems unhappy, ask the question. Ponder it. Look over the principles and pick one that *might* make things better, and try it.

Teach to Learn

Another way to help you learn the material well is to teach it to others. Researchers have been studying what they call "the protégé effect," which is how much better people learn something when they teach it to someone else. Experiments have shown that when students tutor others, they put in extra effort trying to master the material, they remember it with better accuracy, and they're able to apply it better. I think you will find this is true for you too.

Innovative educators are finding practical ways to apply these research results. At the University of Pennsylvania, they've had good results from what they are calling a "cascading mentoring" program where Middle school students are tutored in computer science by high school students, who are themselves tutored by college students.

You can use the same principle yourself when you really want to learn something. If you have a son or a nephew, take it upon yourself to teach him how to make women happy. Teach him about love languages and turning toward bids and oxytocin.

When a buddy of yours says something about his relationship, say something like, "I've been reading this book and it says that your woman can't be happy until you are upset." That's always a way to grab a man's attention. Explain what it means and how it works, and *you* will know it better and find it easier to use your knowledge in your own relationship.

Listen Often

Another good way to solidify your learning is to listen to this on Audible again and again, whenever you're driving. Or listen to it once a month.

According to the International Listening Association, within twenty-four hours, we forget half of any information we've heard. Forty-eight hours later, we will have forgotten 75 percent of it. And we don't grasp everything we hear in the first place.

But these numbers change when what we hear is repeated. And the more it's repeated, the better the numbers look.

You Will Drop This

You will begin to apply some of the ideas in this book, and things will start getting really great between you and your woman, and then it will fade away. When things are going well, you stop trying. This is completely human and totally predictable. The solution is to simply start applying these ideas again.

Rather than deciding that the principles do not work or that you are not capable of applying them or that you lack self-discipline, just realize you are human and that's what humans do. Shrug your shoulders, say to yourself, "Oh well," and start applying the principles again.

Use these methods to master this material and your woman will be happier. You'll see her smile more often. And *you* will be happier too.

About the Author

Adam Khan is the author of the books, *Cultivating Fire, Antivirus For Your Mind, Fill Your Tank With Freedom, Self-Reliance Translated, Slotralogy, Self-Help Stuff That Works, Viewfinder, Principles For Personal Growth*, and *What Difference Does It Make?* See his website at adamlikhan.com.

Adam has been published in Prevention Magazine, Cosmopolitan, Body Bulletin, Wisdom, Your Personal Best Newsletter, Think and Grow Rich Newsletter, the Success Strategies newsletter, and he was a regular columnist for At Your Best (a Rodale Press publication) for seven years where his monthly column was voted the readers' favorite.

www.ingramcontent.com/pod-product-compliance
Lightning Source LLC
Chambersburg PA
CBHW051727040426
42447CB00008B/1018